n+1

ISSUE 25

SPRING 2016

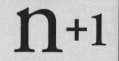

SLOW BURN

ISSUE 25
SPRING 2016

ESSAYS

REVIEWS

LETTERS

Reluctant nationalists and Drake defenders

n+1

n+1 is published three times a year by n+1 Foundation, 68 Jay St. #405, Brooklyn, NY 11201. Single issues are available for $14.95; subscriptions for $36; in Canada and other international, $55. Send correspondence to editors@nplusonemag.com. *n+1* is distributed by Ingram and Ubiquity, Disticor in Canada, and Antenne in the UK and Europe. To place an ad write to ads@nplusonemag.com. *n+1*, Number Twenty-Five © 2016 n+1 Foundation, Inc. ISSN 1549-0033. 978-0-9970318-1-2.

WWW.NPLUSONEMAG.COM

THE INTELLECTUAL SITUATION

A Diary

Bernie's World

FOR THE FIRST SUSTAINED PERIOD IN GENER-ations, it's an exciting time for the American left. While November almost certainly promises the restoration of the Clintons, and significant political victories remain far off, the mood of the country has shifted from the resigned pessimism of the Bush and Obama eras to a kind of bitter, raging "optimism of the will." The brief sunburst of the Occupy protests has left a lasting mark on the language of poverty and inequality and transformed the way the public thinks about finance capitalism. Black Lives Matter has the lips of police chiefs even more spittle-flecked than usual. The prospect of reparations for slavery has, remarkably, become a topic of political consideration. In the space of five years, the avowedly social-ist magazine *Jacobin* has acquired more than sixteen thousand subscribers. Inequality and the costs of globalization are once again up for discussion, even on the right. The train that set off in Seattle in 1999 and was derailed by the war on terror seems to be back on track, and moving at a speedy clip.

Even our endless presidential campaign has its own leftist resurgence in the fig-ure of Bernie Sanders. Although Sanders, a soi-disant socialist, is in most political terms an American liberal, he is *our* liberal, per-haps the first authentically liberal candidate with a shot at the nomination in decades. Many of the things he wants for our domes-tic politics are things the left wants, or would

accept without violent carping: single-payer health care, tighter financial regulation, free public education, a minimum wage on which working people might conceivably live. Moreover, the things Sanders says he wants are, mercifully, the things he actually wants. The neurotic inability to declare one's real beliefs and values, which seems intrinsic to the Democratic Party (see "Politicopsy-chopathology," Issue 15), is alien to Sanders, who has spent his political life largely out-side it.

He has run into difficulties, of course, as with his clumsy early handling of Black Lives Matter and impolitic responses to arguments over reparations. But the impor-tance of these confrontations lies less in Sanders's opinions than in their happen-ing at all. Sanders is the first Democratic candidate in many years to even appear to be responsive to social movements, or to want to encourage their growth. His cam-paign and platform can be criticized profit-ably from the left. It's worth remembering that when Obama's impressively long list of volunteers threatened to become a move-ment, he immediately handed it over to the Democratic National Committee, effectively demobilizing his millions of supporters, whose later protests he condescended to or serenely ignored. If and when Sanders loses the nomination, his supporters may outlive him and his campaign.

But on one significant topic—American foreign policy—Sanders has remained flat-footed. In December, after the shootings in

San Bernardino by self-declared supporters of the Islamic State returned the war on terror to the center of the campaign, Sanders refused to answer questions about ISIS and seemed annoyed that reporters had raised the issue at all. On the Syrian conflict he has been at sea. At that month's Democratic debate he bizarrely referred to Jordan's King Abdullah as a "hero," and in January he called Abdullah "one of the few heroes in a very unheroic place." One doesn't often hear democratic socialists go out of their way to praise hereditary dictators. Sanders has gone further out of his way, repeatedly suggesting that the US strengthen its ties to Saudi Arabia and Qatar. "They have got to start putting some skin in the game," he said in one debate, the theory being that these countries will put up the money and the troops needed to combat extremism in the Middle East, diminishing the American role and thus the opportunity for American malfeasance. Of course the problem is the opposite: both Qatar and Saudi Arabia, two of the US's strongest and least salubrious allies, are already putting lots of money into the Syrian conflict, much of it going to al Qaeda affiliate Jabhat al-Nusra (also supported by the US) and the Islamic State.

Sanders's confusion has often seemed preferable to Hillary Clinton's murderous certainty: as secretary of state she sank an early peace deal in Syria to deepen the US proxy war, and as a candidate has outdone her hawkish self in calling for a no-fly zone, an insane policy that could lead to war with Russia. But Sanders's ultimate lack of a policy doesn't promise an end to the conflict, and it's not always clear that Sanders is as war-averse as he first appears.

As a congressman and senator of twenty-six years, Sanders has a lengthy foreign-policy voting record. That record does little to suggest his views as an independent socialist differ from the Democratic mainstream. He voted for American participation in the Kosovo war in 1999. He supported Israel's 2006 war on Lebanon. He also approved sanctions against Iran and the appropriations bills that have funded our wars in Iraq and Afghanistan. He did join 127 other Congressional Democrats in voting against the invasion of Iraq, but on September 14, 2001, he voted for the Authorization for Use of Military Force, which provides the President and the military with a blank check for war-making on ISIS or any other group judged Islamist and militant. Support for authorization was overwhelming but not unanimous—Sanders could have joined California Democrat Barbara Lee in opposing it. Though Sanders has criticized Clinton for the NATO intervention in Libya, his opposition is somewhat disingenuous: Sanders cosponsored a resolution calling for the ouster of Muammar Qaddafi, which the 2011 bombings accomplished (and more). He also supported the US drone program, though in a more limited form than that in use today.

The alternative to American militarism that Sanders offers is a weak one, the dominant theme a tepid multilateralism. "We cannot and should not be policeman of the world, nor bear the burden of fighting terrorism alone," his website says. "The United States should be part of an international coalition." This is a nice sentiment, but not, after the experience of the last sixteen years, a meaningful one. Obama said that "America is not the world's policeman" in 2013; George W. Bush said, "I don't want to be the world's policeman" in 2000. From Bush's "coalition of the willing" to Obama's fondness for NATO, multilateralism has long been the cheerful mask of American hegemony. Sanders seems ready to do little more than perpetuate it.

How can this be true? Sanders has otherwise been an opponent of American adventurism for decades. During the war in Vietnam, he applied for conscientious-objector status. (His application would be denied, but by then the draft had ended.) In the 1980s, as mayor of Burlington, he was the highest-elected American official to meet with the Sandinistas, whom he supported; he was an ardent opponent of US attempts to destabilize the Nicaraguan government and a foe of the American proxy wars in Latin America more generally. He visited Havana seeking to meet with Castro and honeymooned in the Soviet Union. In one debate with Clinton, he went on a memorable tirade against Henry Kissinger (whom Clinton had cited as a friend and adviser), holding him responsible for the Cambodian genocide because of his support for overthrowing President Sihanouk. ("I am not shocked or surprised by the statement," a Cambodian People's Party spokesman said on learning of Sanders's remarks, "but I am surprised that a foreigner in the US presidential debate is speaking the truth about Cambodian history.")* These are clear signs of a candidate with roots in the solidarity politics of the socialist left—someone for whom anticommunism did not trump all other principles, and for whom anti-imperialism was a principle and a reflex, rather than a mood to be indulged from time to time.

Where is this Sanders now? The failure of the antiwar Sanders to emerge has been roundly criticized in the usual precincts—the late Alexander Cockburn having

prepared the way in column after column ("that brass-lunged fraud from Vermont, Bernard Sanders, 'socialist progressive,' who has endorsed Clinton's bombs"). But perhaps what's missing isn't the anti-imperialist Sanders. It's the antiwar movement he was once part of, and which no longer exists.

Today there is much less public discussion of US actions abroad than when Sanders sought to be a conscientious objector. To be sure, an anti-interventionist mood prevails on the left. But what is missing is a left internationalism worthy of the name—one that envisions a more peaceful and equitable world order, in which the US plays a diminished role. The prospect, however slight, of a Sanders presidency prompts a question: What would a left foreign policy look like? If the left took power, what would it propose? When it comes to the banks, taxes, workplaces, the left's ideas are relatively abundant—they have been furnished by protest movements. As always, social movements affect the party and its likely candidate. But most of our social movements today are turned inward, and have little to say on the fundamental American question affecting the world.

ONE REASON WHY the Sixties antiwar movement continues to be a source of both nostalgia and inspiration for the left is that it had genuine radical potential. Having begun as a movement to stop a war, it nearly became a wholesale revolution that reshaped American politics and foreign policy. It was John Kerry, speaking before the Senate Foreign

---

* When Hillary Clinton pressed Sanders on who his foreign policy advisers were, he harrumphed, "Well, it ain't Kissinger, that's for sure!" As of this writing, it has emerged that Jeffrey Sachs agreed to advise Sanders on foreign policy. As much as Sachs has moved to the left in recent years, a panoply of horrors not altogether dissimilar to Kissinger's might be attributed to him, such as the deployment of mass privatization ("shock therapy") that greatly decreased life expectancy in then de-communizing Russia and Poland, and led to the deaths of millions of people. Sanders's other named policy advisers—Lawrence Korb of the Center for American Progress and Gordon Adams of American University—are unexceptional figures of the defense-policy establishment.

Relations Committee in 1971, who best summed up the movement's aims: "So when thirty years from now our brothers go down the street without a leg, without an arm, or a face, and small boys ask why, we will be able to say 'Vietnam' and not mean a desert, not a filthy obscene memory, but mean instead where America finally turned and where soldiers like us helped it in the turning." That turning never took place: thirty years after Kerry's speech, the war on terror commenced in earnest. Kerry voted in 2001 along with his colleagues Bernie Sanders and Hillary Clinton to invade Afghanistan, and in 2002 with Clinton again to invade Iraq. Just as Kerry abjured his antiwar past as the 2004 presidential candidate—he ran as a war hero, not an antiwar hero—the movement, in the long run, fell far short of its hopes.

The antiwar movement's most dramatic confrontations, the protests outside the 1968 Democratic National Convention in Chicago, were over the party's embrace of the war and its callous nomination of a war-loving candidate. Today, when the Iowa caucuses come into view eleven months before the actual primary, it's difficult to believe that the presumptive Democratic candidate, vice president and Vietnam hawk Hubert Humphrey, achieved the nomination without entering a single primary. (Humphrey was, by polling, the most popular choice among Democrats.) Powerful challenges were mounted by Eugene McCarthy and Robert Kennedy, both antiwar candidates, but one ended in defeat and the other in assassination. The convention was the last in which Democratic delegates were selected through backroom deals and closed caucuses. Outside, the protests against this state of affairs marked the first phase in a transformation of the Democratic Party by the antiwar movement, as well as one

of the movement's lasting legacies. The McGovern-Fraser Commission that followed ushered in the "new politics": affirmative action for party posts, transparency in decision-making. Above all, votes in the primary system would exert more influence over the nomination process than delegates chosen by state committees. The Democratic Party primary system we have today is essentially a result of those days of rage.

But as Daniel Schlozman details in *When Movements Anchor Parties*, the antiwar movement failed both to anchor itself within the party structure and to create a lasting alternative coalition. No national elected official came out of the movement. On its own, the movement fragmented and radicalized, beset by Nixon's repression on the one hand and by faltering strategies on the other. The distinction from the labor movement in the 1930s is enormous. At that time, organized labor, gaining in strength and numbers, weighed working outside the Democratic Party against negotiating with the party for legislative gains and legitimacy. Labor chose the latter strategy. The result was the passage of the National Labor Relations Act and the election of officials who declined to send in troops when workers occupied factories. (This is not to diminish the costs, over time, of being so close to the Democratic Party and blandishments of power, but the benefits were significant.) Nothing comparable occurred with the antiwar movement. By the time its electoral reforms delivered a candidate—George McGovern of McGovern-Fraser—it was too spent a force to work with the candidate. In 1972, McGovern suffered what was then the worst electoral defeat of the postwar era, until Mondale outdid him in 1984.

What could have happened instead? The experience of Chicago proved to many radicals that, in the words of a 1969 *Nation* piece, "the basic institutions of liberal politics—the unions, the convention system, the mass media and the Democratic Party itself—are undemocratic." This was true. But the move to work outside existing vehicles for social transformation left the movement rudderless. The impressive actions against the war—the moratorium, the shutdown of US college campuses after the bombing of Cambodia—likely did spur legislative action. But hostility to the very concepts of parties and institutionalization meant that no lasting alternative emerged. Though some unions were indeed antiwar, they were not routinely mobilized by the New Left as an antiwar force, as they could have been. The big mainstream group, the National Mobilization Committee to End the War, collapsed in the 1970s. What if it had turned instead into an institution dedicated to reevaluating *all* American commitments abroad—something to rival the Council on Foreign Relations? The lasting sour mood over Vietnam suggests that skepticism of American intentions abroad ran deep enough to have made this happen.

The narrow demand to end the war in Vietnam meant that once the Paris Peace Accords were signed in 1973, the movement had little left to pursue beyond the sunlit quadrangles and back-patting panel discussions of academic life. Devious American projects in Central America in the 1980s brought parts of the movement back to life. There were once again victimized parties with which to sympathize, like the National Liberation Front in Vietnam, the FMLN in El Salvador, and the Sandinistas in Nicaragua. These offered the last major opportunities for international solidarity for the descendants of the 1960s American left, as other figures from the movement began their drift toward the Democratic Party right. "Clean for Gene" McCarthy supporters populate

the ranks of the Clintonite hawks, from the odious Lanny Davis (lobbyist for dictators in Honduras, Equatorial Guinea, Ivory Coast, and Bahrain) to Hillary Clinton herself.

What of the spectacular protests against the Iraq war—another opportunity for an anti-imperial project to assert itself and achieve some lasting form? An impressive number of American protesters took to the streets on February 15, 2003, but much smaller countries, such as England, France, and Italy, turned out many more. Here, the anti-Iraq-war contingent remained more mood than movement. Attached to George W. Bush as the Sixties movement was to Vietnam, it had nowhere to go once Bush left office—a departure that only term limits, not the movement itself, could bring about. The two major protest organizations left behind—the ANSWER Coalition and MoveOn—proved likewise feeble, as the former shrank from view and the latter turned into a spammy listserv. When Obama sent more troops to Afghanistan (as promised), vastly expanded the drone assassination program, led a NATO intervention in Libya, and increased CIA-assisted support of "moderate" rebels in Syria while bombing Assad and the Islamic State, there was virtually no opposition, loyal or otherwise.

The difference between policy discussions in the Bush years, during which it was safe to accuse the government of both criminality and insanity, and the Obama years, in which a narrow range of options is presented as the full spectrum of reasonable action (arm the Syrian rebels? Stay the course with a bombing campaign? Send a trickle of "advisers," softly and quietly, to invade Syria?), owes a great deal to the disappearance of the antiwar movement. Like the profession of economics, the field of foreign policy draws its staffers from an elite group of schools and institutions (the Truman

National Security Project, the Woodrow Wilson School at Princeton, the School of Advanced International Studies at Hopkins), whose social-science-trained graduates go into strategic-policy think tanks, congressional staffing jobs, the Departments of State and Defense, and perhaps the White House. But today, while an economist concerned with inequality and distribution can publish the biggest academic best seller of the decade, a foreign-policy expert who presumed that American hegemony was not de facto a good thing would get nowhere, among Democrats and Republicans alike.

Obama's presidency has been in this sense a "return to normalcy," one in which the US's reach continues to grow, now under the safe, capacious awning of foreign-policy "rationality." No more "dumb wars," the memorable phrase with which Obama denounced the Iraq invasion in 2003, still means a lot of wars. As Obama has said of Bush I's national-security adviser, the "realist" Brent Scowcroft, "I love that guy."

THE CONTINUED ABSENCE of an American antiwar movement is especially surprising given the intellectual resources the left has developed since the 1970s. The sense that the US is not a benign actor in the world is now commonly understood, and an awareness of the stupidity of numerous US interventions—from Mossadegh in 1953 to Libya in 2011—distinguishes most left-wing commentary on US foreign policy from its more superficially respectable counterparts. Even if Sanders is proof that knowledge of the US's bad decisions is not bulwark enough against supporting more bad decisions, the attempt to produce a critical mind-set about bombing other countries has been a valuable one.

Among the most tireless skeptics of US interventions is Noam Chomsky, who may also be the greatest intellectual gift the movement left behind. Chomsky has been a fixture of the antiwar left for so long that it's hard to recall his startling emergence from academic linguistics into the ranks of Sixties radicals. "A slim sharp-featured man with an ascetic expression, and an air of gentle but absolute moral integrity" was how Norman Mailer described him in *Armies of the Night*, recalling when he and Chomsky shared a jail cell after a protest at the Pentagon. His constancy has made him difficult to appreciate sufficiently; he is the Tim Duncan of intellectual life. But to read Chomsky's writing—from the careful rebuttals of official nonsense on Vietnam to the magisterial "Responsibility of Intellectuals" to the many interviews and articles he published leading up to, and following, the Iraq debacle—is to see a relentlessly intelligent mind.

Chomsky is a generous person, if not always to his opponents, and perhaps his most generous contribution to political thought is his willingness to sift through tedious reams of so-called realist foreign-policy thinking to reveal its utter unreality, so that others don't have to. From Chomsky's point of view, supposedly hard-bitten, uncompromising realists like Kissinger appear as the true madmen of history. (Kissinger in 1963: "In the decades ahead, the West will have to lift its sights to encompass a more embracing concept of reality. . . . There are two kinds of realists: those who manipulate facts and those who create them. The West requires nothing so much as men able to create their own reality.")

Chomsky's staying power is partly due to the simplicity of his response to nearly every ludicrous foreign-policy initiative the US has put forward. It is essentially, as Bruce Robbins has noted in a penetrating essay, a version of the Golden Rule: Treat others as you would be treated. "The standards we apply to others," Chomsky has written, "we must apply to ourselves." So regarding the US drug war in Colombia, Chomsky can write: "Imagine the reaction to a proposal that Colombia or China should undertake fumigation programs in North Carolina to destroy government-subsidized crops used for more lethal products." Chomsky compares the rationale for the American "preventive" invasion of Vietnam to the Japanese preventive bombing of Pearl Harbor. When Chomsky says, as he has repeatedly, that "the US itself is a leading terrorist state," he not only confounds and deeply irritates his opponents but elucidates the emptiness of the political attack on "terror" as such. Isn't precision bombing terror? Are the lives of civilians terrorized and murdered in Peshawar by American drone strikes worth less than the lives lost on September 11? The force and clarity of Chomsky's thinking has become so reliable that we have lost the ability to appreciate it.

Yet the hegemony of Chomskyism has hobbled the internationalist left in one respect. For if Chomsky is invaluable as a critic of the US (and by extension Israel), he is less valuable as a critic of any other state. Chomsky's internationalism is a kind of Americanism: When the US does it, it's likely to be bad. This is, of course, usually true. Of the interventions Chomsky has opposed in recent years—Afghanistan, Iraq (twice), Libya—he has had ample cause, and the results have spoken for themselves. But on intervention by other states, he has been equivocal, or even assenting. Regarding the Indian intervention in then East Pakistan in 1971, and the Vietnamese invasion of Cambodia in 1978, he expressed partial approval, because each helped to halt mass murders (though the primary goals were by no means humanitarian); equally gratifying to

Chomsky may have been the fact that both were carried out against US wishes. Still, though India was not *the* world hegemon, it was certainly a hegemon. Indira Gandhi used the pretext of the intervention, and the fact of having soldiers massed on the border between West Bengal and East Pakistan, to round up twenty thousand Maoists in India. Her intervention in another country thus enabled a repressive counterinsurgency at home. Was the intervention justifiable then? The guides to thinking through this problem are not within Chomsky's purview.*

Chomsky's American antistatism—bracing and helpful as it has been—sometimes makes other kinds of internationalism difficult. If the temptation facing one set of political figures is to wake up every morning wondering whom to bomb next, the temptation facing the left is to keep one's hands clean; to withdraw from the world, taking up an older but no less simplistic approach to foreign policy, isolationism à la George Washington and Ron Paul. Maybe that is the most honorable position, the least susceptible to mealymouthedness and hypocrisy. But so long as the seeking of national political office, the taking of state power, continues to be a goal of the left, it is incumbent on us to figure out what we *might* do—what *ought* to happen should some Chomsky-like figure (Bernie!) happen to find himself attaining the presidency.

AGGRESSIVE EXPANSION has been a practice of the United States at least since the Louisiana Purchase and the decline of the Federalist Party, which opposed Jefferson's massive land grab. By the end of the 19th century, concomitant with the spectacular growth of US industrial power and the seizure of far-flung territories like Hawaii and

*It should be said that Chomsky was a signatory to a 1974 letter protesting Gandhi's torture of Maoist prisoners.

the Philippines, a foreign policy extending beyond the Western Hemisphere began to emerge. Secretary of State John Hay's "Open Door" proposals in 1899, regarding the importance of keeping Chinese markets open, were an early statement of American attitudes toward foreign markets. The US, the occupation of the Pacific Islands notwithstanding, remained ambivalent about formal colonialism; it largely pursued access to markets not by building an imperial trading bloc but through free-trade policies that favored its own markets, backed by the implicit threat of force.

As Perry Anderson argued recently in a pair of articles for the *New Left Review*, it was only with the end of World War II and the onset of the cold war that the American attitude toward global hegemony shifted from improvisation to deep coherence. Confronted with a rival for world influence that explicitly sought the elimination of capitalism, the US constructed a different model of geopolitical grand strategy. The US would allow Japan's and Germany's markets to be reconstructed along protectionist lines (while housing American military bases). This was antithetical to "Open Door" ideas of free markets, but adjunct to the American attempt to extend its influence and power across the globe. It was not American capitalism that the US would protect, but *capital* as such. Anderson: "The US state would henceforward act, not primarily as a projection of the concerns of US capital, but as a guardian of the general interest of all capitals, sacrificing—where necessary, and for as long as needed—national gain for international advantage."

To be sure, the US would not be above fighting to maintain supremacy in Far Eastern theaters, or shy of deposing leaders. The US saw the cold war as both an existential struggle and a matter of simple international

strategy, and acquired advantages where it could. But overall, its aims were to maintain the economic stability of states within the international order—an order with the US at its head. The "new world order" that came into existence after the dissolution of the Soviet Union was not, in fact, so new at all. The US simply cemented its position as the world hegemon, without which no stable order could exist. The keyword of this order has always been *security*, often accompanied by the qualifier *national*. It is this idea—that American power is to ensure the security of free markets and peoples by any means necessary—that a left foreign policy ought to dismantle.

American foreign policy—Obama's not excepted—has sought to exert control in the name of protecting Americans and the international order. Endless apocalyptic threats, from without and within, have spurred belligerent American expansion and military buildup. Harry Truman's March 1947 speech against the threat of communism in Greece, essentially outlining the Truman Doctrine, was designed, in the words of the Senate Foreign Relations Committee chairman Arthur Vandenberg, "to scare the hell out of the country." Soon thereafter, Congress approved the first great global application of American economic power, the Marshall Plan. Fearmongering leading to force has been a leitmotif of American life ever since: no country so rich and placid has been so disproportionately overwhelmed by a sense of impending terror (especially after the risk of full-scale nuclear exchange declined in the 1960s). After the establishment of the Sandinista government in Nicaragua, Reagan sonorously warned Americans that a Soviet beachhead lay "only two hours' flying time from our own borders." Since 2001, of course, the sense of threat has been magnified beyond belief—even though neither al Qaeda (our partners in Syria) nor the Islamic State pose an existential danger to the US or even its allies.

The obvious response to the arguments in favor of heightened national security is that every expansive step in the war on terror has made the US and the world increasingly *less* safe; that in pursuit of "security," security itself has been compromised. The pursuit of extraregional hegemony by the US has been a disaster, unmotivated and unnecessary. The multiplication of actual threats and violence to countries everywhere has been the consequence.

But to charge that security politics has produced insecurity is to give legitimacy to security politics. The real first step to a left foreign policy is simply to acknowledge the following: US hegemony not only has been a moral and human catastrophe but also is in decline. What US policy has masked is the growth of world powers besides the US. The decline of US hegemony was already visible during the Bush Administration, when Latin American countries, led by Brazil, began to seek alliances with Iran, Russia, and China. It has become obvious in the Syrian Civil War, which several powers—Iran, Russia, Turkey, Saudi Arabia, and Qatar—have been exploiting to pursue ends hostile to each other and often to the US (which is itself unwilling or incapable of exerting influence the way it might have years ago).

To imagine a world in which American primacy is no longer taken for granted requires a scaling back of aims and a deconstruction of the project of "security." It requires, above all, a slow and steady revision of the American worldview, in which the presumption of leadership has been discarded, and a new, less hospitable order has been accepted.

Such an intellectual shift would require a realistic reckoning with what forces for liberation exist in the world, without extravagant hopes or illusions—call it a "left realism." Does this mean that a nation must refuse to "intervene," that a respect for the nation-state and its sovereignty trumps all? It doesn't, and the historical record contains many instances where a timely intervention might have halted a war: for example, against the Germans prior to the invasion of Poland. But the record is more full of overweening, preventive actions that prolonged and augmented catastrophe, such as the British intervention in World War I, when a swift German victory over France might have been preferable.

What has clearly been a force for instability has been the presumption that US-led forces will always be ready to intervene when a country seems poised to slaughter its own citizens. The case of Libya is exemplary. When the Arab Spring reached Benghazi, Qaddafi's forces launched a counteroffensive and appeared to the US, as well as France and Britain, on the verge of slaughter. But the conflict was heightened because the rebel forces assumed—correctly, as it happened—that the US and its allies would intervene. As Rajan Menon pointed out last year in an excellent realist article in the *National Interest*, there were no efforts to pursue nonmilitary steps between February 18, when the uprising began, and March 17, when the no-fly zone was declared. Why? Libya was a weak state, with a decrepit military and few allies in the region. The intervention, followed by a sly enlargement of goals to include the removal of Qaddafi, would offend no one. (This is presumably why Hillary Clinton found it OK to joke about his death—"We came, we saw, he died"—with classic American vulgarity.) What would happen if the Arab Spring came to Saudi Arabia, a state as repressive and undemocratic as Qaddafi's Libya?

The same thing that has happened with Turkey's murder of thousands of Kurdish civilians since 1984, or Russia's flattening of Grozny: nothing.

A similar pattern of intervention seemed at hand at the beginning of the Syrian conflict, when Obama declared Assad's use of sarin gas a "red line." Based on this rhetoric, and what happened in Libya, the opposition to Assad expected that the US would forcefully intervene in the way that it had in Libya. But both the US and the rebels miscalculated. Syria had an ally in the region, Iran, and a much larger ally outside the region, Russia, which had bases on Syrian soil. Russia, it turned out, had also been offended by NATO's overthrow of Qaddafi. Putin would not countenance the same action against Assad. The result was a mirror of the lead-up to Qaddafi's overthrow, and then a sudden reversal: the determination of the armed opposition led to an increase in bloodshed, but no help came. A peace deal in 2012 that might have led to Assad's departure was scuttled by Western powers, under the idea that Assad's fall was imminent. It wasn't. A rebellion turned into a civil war, which turned into a massive proxy war of regional and extra-regional powers, a spiral of death only recently paused by a belated cease-fire. No clearer instance of the limits of both American power and political romanticism exists than now in Syria. But beyond this sobering fact, the conflict has offered little in the way of clarity for the left. No settlement will be satisfying or humane. The only option is to support peace, virtually at any cost.

This has not stopped some on the left from seeking more traditional kinds of solidarity. Much of the critique of American foreign policy over the cold war years was buoyed by support for leftist governments or movements, from the Cuban revolution to Nicaragua. Though such movements have grown sparse with the decline of decolonization and international socialism, today an analogous glimmer comes from the state of Rojava in northern Syria, where, improbably enough, local Kurds have founded an egalitarian society inspired by the work of the American anarchist Murray Bookchin, transmitted through the prison writings of Kurdistan Workers' Party founder Abdullah Öcalan. Support for this movement has been strong on the Anglo-American left (rightly so), above all in the writings of David Graeber, who has compared the situation of the Rojava revolutionaries to that of the anarchists in the Spanish Civil War—and argues that they should receive similar support.

But such thinking can easily lead to the embrace of a military solution centered on the US: the Al Jazeera English (and generally antiwar) reporter Mehdi Hassan and (more predictably) Joel Gillin of the *New Republic* have argued for arming Kurdish rebels. American airstrikes have already been helping Kurdish forces combat the Islamic State, which at the time of this writing is on the verge of defeat in Syria. But what then? The Kurds are only being used by American powers as a tool: if and when ISIS in Syria is defeated, their American support will dry up. They can't move outside their territory, and they won't topple Assad. And it is absolutely right—imperative, even—for social movements in the US to support democratic allies against Assad. But a left foreign policy cannot simply mean backing any leftist project that happens to come along.

We should be circumspect in our enthusiasms not least because US involvement in Syria has served a broader and older goal: the war on terror. This war, with its omnipresent surveillance and planet-spanning assassinations, represents the most massive expansion of American militarism under the rubric of "security" since the beginning of the cold war. Reflexive interventionism has only been augmented by the rationale of a conflict whose ambit is everywhere. With drone strikes and support to allies bombing others (such as the Saudi war on the Houthis in Yemen), the US is intervening all the time. Nixon's 1968 campaign slogan, "Peace with honor," has been traded for war without end.

The consensus around intervention—often called, after a 2001 UN commission, the "Responsibility to Protect"—has become intimately bound up with the war on terror. The project of any leftist government would start here, by dismantling both the war apparatus and the presumption that the US's existence is predicated on guaranteed intervention. Amazingly, it is Obama himself, in the sunset of his otherwise frustrating and belligerent presidency, who has begun to seek out ways to change the attitude of the "international community" toward intervention. In this respect, the characteristic Obama is not the one who declared a red line, but the one who largely refused to act on it and has rejected calls to do more. This is the same President who privately has taken to calling Libya a "shit show." Fine words, but it's his shit show. A left presidency would be one in which this realistic appraisal would come as a matter of habit, rather than after months or years of prevarication and worse.

A movement to end the war on terror—resuming the project of the peace movement of the Sixties—would be only the beginning of a left foreign policy. Take, for instance, the "Pivot to Asia," a military buildup around China that has the eventual goal of deploying 60 percent of all Navy and Air Force units to the region. Eighty thousand US soldiers are already stationed in South Korea and Japan. The stated reason for this massing of forces is the militarization of the region by China—but it seems just as likely that any buildup by China is responding to the long and increasing domination of the region by the US.

In other words, to look beyond one war is to see the next one looming. For a real left foreign policy, "containing China" would no longer present itself as axiomatic, because *security* would no longer be the watchword of everyday life. It would, instead, be *peace*. +

JENNIFER MURPHY, *BUTTERFLY SKULL*. 2010, PAPER AND THREAD. COURTESY CLINT ROENISCH GALLERY.

POLITICS

Memoranda

GEORGE BLAUSTEIN
Miracles and Mummeries

LATE IN LIFE, THOMAS JEFFERSON TOOK A
razor to his King James Bible and cut out all
the nice parts from the Gospels: Christ's life
and death, the Sermon on the Mount, the
parables, the Golden Rule. He pasted those
parts alongside corresponding Greek, Latin,
and French translations and gave the world
The Life and Morals of Jesus of Nazareth.
Gone are the angels, the miracles, Christ's
divinity, the resurrection, anything supernatural. What's left is a clean and ethical
extraction. (You can still read the chaff at the
Smithsonian: Jefferson kept his carved-up
King James intact, like the preserved skeleton of a vanished species.) For Antonin
Scalia, this arrogant violation made Jefferson the first activist judge. It is cowardly and
ungrateful to cut out the parts you don't like,
to take the good without the bad.

Scalia's antipathy to the Jefferson Bible,
which he expressed in a 1996 speech at the
Mississippi College of Law, was key to his
variety of "originalism," the philosophy of
constitutional interpretation with which he
was most associated. Originalism insists
on interpreting the Constitution as it was
understood at the time of its ratification, but
this definition only raises questions: about
whose understanding matters, about the
virtues and vices of the framers, about the
framers' intentions versus the text's public

meaning, about whether our responsibility
is to 18th-century language or 18th-century
values, about whether we can know the past
at all. The clearest thing one can say about
originalism is that it opposes the idea of a
"living Constitution." Beyond that, it is a
label that obscures a great many contradictions within the ranks of conservative
jurisprudence.

SCALIA'S ORIGINALISM was a form of self-
abnegation consistent with the ritual self-
abnegations of Catholic history. It says to
the interpreter, don't be led into temptation, but it acknowledges how tempting
those temptations can be. (Not for nothing did Robert H. Bork, the first originalist martyr—and later a convert to Catholicism—title his book *The Tempting of
America: The Political Seduction of the Law.*)
Who wouldn't want to carve up the Bible
and ignore the hard parts? Who wouldn't
want to extrapolate a general right to privacy from the rights specifically mentioned
in the Constitution? (In *Griswold v. Connecticut* [1965], Justice William O. Douglas
found that general right in the Constitution's "penumbras" and "emanations"—the
kind of vocabulary, and decision, that
originalists despise.) Who wouldn't want
to believe that the Constitution *lives*, that
its meaning evolves as our own sensibili-
ties and technologies evolve, that the old
We the People who wrote and ratified the
Constitution includes the modern We the
People, too? Alas, the living Constitution

is a false miracle: "The Constitution that I interpret and apply," Scalia wrote in 2002, "is not living but dead—or, as I prefer to put it, enduring." Originalism kills the Constitution so that the Constitution can endure, so that the Constitution won't betray itself.

To be an originalist is to be surrounded by temptations. It is certainly tempting to suggest, as the liberal Warren Court suggested in *Brown v. Board of Education* (1954), that "we cannot turn the clock back to 1868, when the [14th] Amendment was adopted," but rather have to "consider public education in the light of its full development and its present place in American life throughout the Nation." The originalist says that we *can* turn back the clock, and we must, because the text demands it—even when our modern antiracist, integrationist pieties would prefer not to. Even to claim the mantle of "higher law"—as emancipatory movements often have, from abolitionism to civil rights—is itself a temptation. While the citizen might be able to indulge in such pleasures without ruining the state, the originalist judge is bound by what's written. He is a priest who reads, not a prophet who writes.

In theory, this sort of originalism allows no imagination, because most of the time, originalists consider the text's historical meaning to be self-evident—a "piece of cake," as Scalia said. Naturally, this raises the hackles of academic historians (like me) who are obliged to insist that history is hard, or at least theoretically and epistemologically interesting. But Scalia was charismatic in his confidence about the transparency of the past. One of the "false notions" refuted in *Reading Law*, his handbook, is the idea that "lawyers and judges, not being historians, are unqualified to do the historical research that originalism requires." Judges do history all the time! In a 2006 debate between Scalia and Justice Stephen Breyer, Breyer (a liberal

advocate of the "living Constitution") said that if historical truth was all that mattered, then "we should have nine historians on the court" and be done with it. Scalia's response was that nine historians—even amateur historians—would be better than nine ethicists. And indeed his originalism was not an ethics: it was a refusal to participate in ethics.

Perhaps this is why Scalia was such a good writer. The imagination that originalism did not demand was funneled into his prose, which had the bite of Tory satire and the grandeur of Counter-Reformation polemic. His dissents drip with disdain for liberalism as a false church. At times he condemned judicial activism the way the early church condemned Gnostic heresies: "What secret knowledge," he sarcastically mused in a 1996 case about whether the government could hire or fire someone on the basis of that person's political views, "is breathed into lawyers when they become Justices of this Court, that enables them to discern that a practice which the text of the Constitution does not clearly proscribe, and which our people have *regarded* as constitutional for 200 years, is in fact unconstitutional?" In 2015's landmark gay-marriage case, Justice Anthony Kennedy aligned the high court with "the highest ideals of love, fidelity, devotion, sacrifice, and family," and with "a love that may endure even past death." But Scalia scoffed at these "mummeries and straining-to-be-memorable passages." Mummery! A nice old word for a "ridiculous ceremony (formerly used esp. of religious ritual regarded as pretentious or hypocritical)," or the "extravagant costume or other paraphernalia associated with or worthy of such ceremony," according to the *Oxford English Dictionary*. Mummery is a word early Protestants hurled at Catholics; Scalia turned the tables, and hurled the 16th-century insult at a 21st-century liberal tear-jerker. His obscurer insults—argle-bargle, jiggery-pokery—have a similar Elizabethan whiff, though they are newer coinages.

Miracles

IS IT STRANGE THAT THE HIGHEST COURT IN the land is all Catholics and Jews? American Protestants of an earlier age would have choked on their graham crackers. Is it stranger or less strange that when the new pope addressed Congress, three of the six Catholics didn't show up? Antonin Scalia is an illuminating figure to follow through the recent history of American religion and politics, for his career was both illustrative and idiosyncratic. To read him within and against that history will require a few tangents, some religious stereotyping, and some conspiratorial thinking.

Scalia had nine children (a nice Court-size number), and he drove an extra hour to the Cathedral of St. Matthew the Apostle so he could hear the Latin Mass. "The kid was a conservative when he was 17 years old. An archconservative Catholic," a former classmate told the *New York Times* in 1986, when Scalia was nominated. "He could have been a member of the Curia." If Jefferson was Scalia's villain, his hero was Sir Thomas More, the great opponent of the Protestant Reformation in England and the patron saint of lawyers. In Nelson Shanks's 2007 portrait of Scalia, an image of More peeks out from beneath a book on the desk. Scalia even wore a replica of More's iconic hat to Barack Obama's second inaugural. More's last words—"I die the king's good servant but God's first"—were read, fittingly, at Scalia's funeral.

Scalia was not the first Catholic justice, but a certain Catholic sensibility became jurisprudentially interesting with his ascent.

The first Catholic justice was Roger Taney, chief justice from 1836 to 1864. He was a Jacksonian Democrat, remembered now for the disastrous *Dred Scott v. Sandford*, which drew on the framers' original intention to give black people no rights whatsoever, and accelerated the coming of the Civil War. In the 20th century, there was an unofficial "Catholic seat" alongside the better-known "Jewish seat" inaugurated by Louis Brandeis in 1916. The import of both seats was demographic rather than theological or ideological: in 1986, Scalia's Queens-marinated Italian-Americanness was more noteworthy than his preference for the Latin Mass. This was soon after the emergence of the so-called Reagan Democrat—working-class white ethnics who gravitated toward the Republican Party and away from their economic interests. Senate Democrats, spooked by this supposed exodus, didn't want to antagonize Italian-Americans, or Queens, by resisting Scalia's nomination. But soon Catholicism became less a matter of demographics or representation—both Catholics and Jews being bizarrely well represented ever since—and more a matter of ideology.

One moment from Scalia's career stands out to me as particularly revealing. In 1996, he gave a speech at the Mississippi College of Law—a private Southern Baptist institution. The speech led to some grumpy liberal op-eds, because it was not customary for a Supreme Court justice to encourage his listeners to be "fools for Christ's sake" (invoking Paul to the Corinthians), or to "pray for the courage to endure the scorn of the sophisticated world."

It was also unusual for a justice to discuss religious miracles, as Scalia did that day—and as he would in later years, usually before Catholic audiences. In 2001, about secular media: "Even if a miracle occurred under their noses, they would not believe."

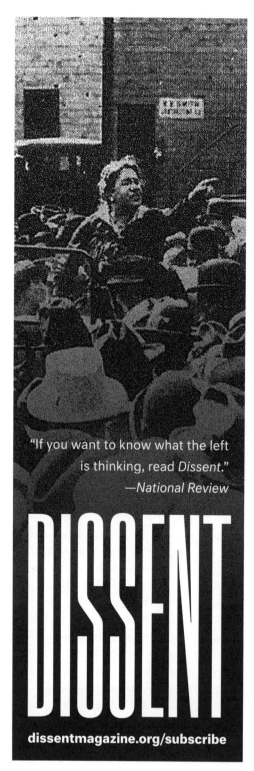

In 2005, to the Knights of Columbus: "Intellect and reason need not be laid aside for religion. It is not irrational to accept the testimony of eyewitnesses who had nothing to gain. There is something wrong with rejecting a priori the existence of miracles." And in 2010, to the St. Thomas More Society, which gave him the replica hat: "A faith that has no rational basis is a false faith. . . . What is irrational is to reject . . . the possibility of miracles in general and of the resurrection of Jesus Christ in particular."

As a matter of faith, Scalia believed in miracles (as I do). As a matter of logic, he insisted (as I would) that belief in miracles is rational, while a priori nonbelief in miracles is irrational. He pushed back against the "worldly wise"—intellectuals, journalists, academics—who "just will not have anything to do with miracles." This erasure of the miraculous was another reason Scalia couldn't stand the Jefferson Bible, back to which, in the same speech, he traced the history of this current of self-serving skepticism. The Southern Baptist lawyers in training gave him a standing ovation.

That may seem unsurprising now, but the Baptists' ovation strikes me as far stranger than a Catholic justice's contrarian but earnest belief in miracles. For how could a Southern Baptist in good conscience acknowledge the Catholic statues that miraculously wept in a Virginia suburban church, or the painful stigmata that appeared on the resident priest's wrists? (The particular miracle that Scalia mentioned was the 1992 case of Father Jim Bruse.) Not so long ago, a good Protestant would have dismissed this as Romish superstition. And on the other side, Scalia's argument against a priori rejection of miracles was originally a Catholic argument deployed against Protestants. Is there nothing to be said for denominational distinction? Has ideological polarization so trumped questions of theology that Catholics and Southern Baptists can harmoniously lie down together, lion and lamb, as conservative bedfellows?

THAT EPISODE of Baptists' applauding a Catholic's weeping statues is a vivid miniature of the alliance of evangelical Protestants and conservative Catholics that shapes this country's conservative politics. We might be witnessing the first rumblings of its collapse, so now is a good time to pay our respects to it. Nixon brought part of the "Catholic vote" into the Republican coalition, siphoning anti-abortionists from the Democratic Party's fraying New Deal coalition in the early 1970s. Alongside that story runs a current of intellectual and theological history that inflected Scalia's constitutional moment more directly and forms the context of his religious invocations. The rapprochement between evangelicals and Catholics is best captured by a manifesto from 1994: "Evangelicals & Catholics Together: The Christian Mission in the Third Millennium." It was signed by fifteen dignitaries—clergy, ministers, theologians, heads of ministries and missions—from both sides of the Reformation's narrowing aisle. It was endorsed by bright lights of Christian academia, like the historians Mark Noll and Nathan Hatch, and by dimmer but far-reaching lights of the Christian right, like former presidential candidate Pat Robertson.

The main authors were Father Richard John Neuhaus and Chuck Colson. Colson was an old Nixon hand who found God shortly before going to prison for his involvement in Watergate. Neuhaus had written *The Naked Public Square: Religion and Democracy and America* (1984), which lamented the secularization of American public life and the privatization of religion. Formerly a Lutheran pastor, Neuhaus

followed the road to Rome in 1990, the same year he founded the journal *First Things*, which remains the major intellectual outlet of conservative Christianity (and which published "Evangelicals & Catholics Together").

This document remains the clearest and soberest statement of conservative Christian ecumenism. These traditional rivals gathered in a Venn diagram of common beliefs ("a free economy," "parental choice in education," "Western culture") and joined forces against Christendom's common enemies (abortion, militant secularism masquerading as multiculturalism, pornography, "antireligious bigotry in the entertainment media," public funding for art like *Piss Christ*). In a reactionary, restorationist mode, the signers agreed to "contend together for a renewal of the constituting vision of the place of religion in the American experiment."

The things that evangelicals and Catholics disagree about—grace versus works, symbolism versus transubstantiation, remembrance of Mary versus devotion to Mary, "the sole authority of Scripture (*sola scriptura*)" versus "Scripture as authoritatively interpreted in the church"—were, for the time being, put aside. Perhaps one could read about them in the journal *Second Things*, which does not exist, but should. The new allies also agreed to stop "sheep stealing"—proselytizing across the evangelical/Catholic divide. There were more than enough sheep fleeing the liberal mainline Protestant denominations.

This alliance grounded itself in a variety of originalism different from Scalia's. This originalism looked to the American revolutionary generation and the Constitution's framers for "moral truth": "With the Founders of the American experiment, we declare, 'We hold these truths.' With them, we hold that this constitutional order is composed not just of rules and procedures but is most essentially a moral experiment." Consider the First Amendment, which protects the "free exercise" of "religion" against congressional infringement. According to the originalism of First Thingers, this is a protection of religion against nonreligion, not a "wall of separation between Church & State." (That phrase is not in the Constitution; it's Jefferson's renegade metaphor from a letter to some Connecticut Baptists.) The First Amendment's prohibition of an "establishment of religion" implied no sanction against religion; rather, it marked a compromise among religiously diverse states, some of which still had state-level religious establishments. This is why the alliance rejoiced at the 2014 case *Burwell v. Hobby Lobby Stores, Inc.*, in which the conservative wing of the court (all Catholic) imputed religious beliefs to corporate "persons" and unburdened the Pentecostal owners of Hobby Lobby of the Affordable Care Act's "contraception mandate." When that case was decided, *First Things* suggested that Neuhaus was "smiling down from heaven."

This alliance embraced Scalia as its hero on the court. *First Things* has eulogized him as "Our Mighty Rearguard." But I can imagine him shrugging at this insistence on "moral truths" and "moral experiments," even while he basically went along with it. His originalism demanded submission, not moral heroism. It did not insist on the Constitution's moral content, only its semantic stasis. Scalia's Constitution is not a sacred text, after all: a sacred text might be open to sectarian dispute, and Scalia's is not. By contrast, Hugo Black, an originalist *avant la lettre*, famously carried a copy of the Constitution in his pocket, the way a Protestant fundamentalist carries a dog-eared Bible. And Black was a bastion of the liberal Warren Court who inventively deployed originalist arguments to liberal ends, invoking the framers' intentions as if

they were morally visionary. Scalia was different. His Constitution has authority not because it is holy, not because the vision of its authors was moral, but because it is the Constitution.

There is satisfaction in tautology. A constitution has what Scalia called an "antievolutionary purpose," and to suggest that its meaning could evolve was, in his eyes, to throw away the only thing that could possibly serve as a rudder: "Perhaps the most glaring defect of Living Constitutionalism, next to its incompatibility with the whole antievolutionary purpose of a constitution, is that there is no agreement, and no chance of agreement, upon what is to be the guiding principle of the evolution," he wrote in 1997. "As soon as the discussion goes beyond the issue of whether the Constitution is static, the evolutionists divide into as many camps as there are individual views of the good, the true, and the beautiful." The Constitution governs not because it is *intrinsically* good, true, or beautiful. It isn't. It governs because it is an institution, in the form of a document, which "We the People" agreed would not evolve. For Scalia, having a rock is a lot better than not having a rock.

MARRIAGES OF CONVENIENCE often end in divorce. The evangelical-Catholic marriage might, too. The new pope—a social-gospel progressive of an older Catholic style—has undermined the ideological premises of "Evangelicals & Catholics Together." Francis is theologically as Catholic as, well, the pope, but he has prioritized poverty, human migration, and the environment over the culture-warring of his predecessors and of the United States Conference of Catholic Bishops. Second things have a way of becoming first things again, and suddenly the future of Catholicism looks quite different than it did even three years ago. And intra-Catholic crises rise again to the surface, as conservative Catholics, bereft of the conservative magisterium of John Paul II and Benedict XVI, scramble to other bulwarks of orthodoxy. These tensions enter American politics in bizarre ways, as when some clever conservative saboteurs maneuvered the pope into the same room with the Kentucky county clerk (Kim Davis—a *Pentecostal* county clerk) who had refused to issue gay-marriage licenses.

The unholy alliance might fray for internal American reasons as well. Consider the religious pluralism of the Republican Party, if *pluralism* is the right word. In 2012, both vice-presidential candidates were Catholics: Joe Biden from the old-guard Irish Catholic wing of the Democratic coalition, Paul Ryan from the newer wing of Catholics who read Ayn Rand. The Republican candidate was a Mormon, which was a difficult pill for the Huckabees (Southern Baptist) and Santorums (Catholic) to swallow. It is easy to forget how hostile evangelical Christians were to Romney, particularly in the South. But what a miracle that the Grand Old Party—founded, historically, by antislavery, frequently anti-Catholic, and *definitely* anti-Mormon Protestants in the 1850s; currently home to a white, evangelical, generally antipluralist "base"—gave American politics its first non-"Protestant" presidential ticket ever. (That is, if we don't see Mormonism

as a Protestant denomination. When Romney was nominated, Billy Graham's website had to remove Mormonism from its list of cults.) And ultimately, the only one of the final four to have told of an evangelical-Protestant conversion experience, albeit obliquely, was Barack Obama, in his account of joining Chicago's Trinity United Church of Christ in *Dreams from My Father.**

In the current Republican primaries, the Southern Baptist (Ted Cruz) attacked the cradle Catholic (Marco Rubio) while the Catholic convert (Jeb Bush) withered on the vine. They all claim Scalia as their favorite justice. Donald Trump (technically Presbyterian, but only in a way that calls to mind the old joke that Presbyterians are Methodists with money) clashes with the pope over the unity of mankind and hints that Scalia was murdered. Wrecking the alliance of conservative Christianity and conservative politics would be the only thing for which Trump could conceivably be applauded. That alliance has been bad for Christianity and bad for conservatism.

American religious-political alliances almost always involve strange bedfellowships and Faustian bargains. This is what makes American politics interesting for a historian of religion. And it gives the United States a place in larger, cosmic dramas of the divine and demonic. If I have called for a renewal of interdenominational strife (a strange

---

* "And in that single note—hope!—I heard something else; at the foot of that cross, inside the thousands of churches across the city, I imagined the stories of ordinary black people merging with the stories of David and Goliath, Moses and Pharaoh, the Christians in the lion's den, Ezekiel's field of dry bones. Those stories—of survival, and freedom, and hope—became our story, my story; the blood that had spilled was our blood, the tears our tears; until this black church, on this bright day, seemed once more a vessel carrying the story of a people into future generations and into a larger world. . . . As the choir lifted back up into song, as the congregation began to applaud those who were walking to the altar to accept Reverend Wright's call, I felt a light touch on the top of my hand. I looked down to see the older of the two boys sitting beside me, his face slightly apprehensive as he handed me a pocket tissue. Beside him, his mother glanced at me with a faint smile before turning back toward the altar. It was only as I thanked the boy that I felt the tears running down my cheeks.

"'Oh, Jesus,' I heard the older woman beside me whisper softly. 'Thank you for carrying us this far.'"

argument, I admit), it is only because I don't want the ideological certainties of this world to pollute or dilute theological seriousness. Conservative clamors about "religious freedom" have, perversely, only hastened the secularization of intellectual life, by painting "religion" into a corner of anti-intellectualism and victimology. An ideologically rigid defense of "religion" narrows and tarnishes what it tries to defend, and leaves out everything that is powerful and true and sacred about religious experience.

Duresse Oblige

THE SUPREME COURT IS OUR HOLY SEE. The court promises stability, tradition, and ancient-sounding Latin rituals. In costumes of somber glory, it speaks ex cathedra on the meaning of the Constitution, and for some reason we believe it has the authority to do so. *Marbury v. Madison* is our First Vatican Council. Judicial review resembles papal infallibility, and is, in the end, as fragile as papal infallibility (although we rarely reflect on that fragility). The nomination of a Supreme Court justice is the closest thing the United States has to the election of a pope: from an extremely narrow pool of judicial cardinals and insiders comes a new statesman in robes. He (usually he) is presented to the public in the Rose Garden, America's balcony of St. Peter's, ready to assume a lifetime position. His face will be new to most of the millions who are now his flock, but his every past action and utterance will be combed for clues to our future.

Then come the twin gauntlets of democratic interrogation and popular spectacle, and the analogy falters. The new pope is insulated from questions about how "a wise Latina woman" might rule differently from "a white male who hasn't lived that life." But

other analogies surface—martyrdom, for instance, or sainthood. Remember Chief Justice John Roberts's unblinking eyes in his Senate confirmation hearings? They were like the judicial version of Renée Falconetti's eyes in Carl Dreyer's *Passion of Joan of Arc*. Clarence Thomas (a Catholic who considered entering the priesthood) called the allegations against him a "high-tech lynching," but they allowed him to perform the role of a would-be martyr.

The first originalist martyr was Robert H. Bork, the arch-conservative judge nominated by Ronald Reagan a year after Scalia's ascent and rejected by the Senate in a dramatic standoff—an episode that left us *bork* as a verb. Bork, who called himself an atheist when he was nominated and rejected, converted to Catholicism only after this original borking. Anthony Kennedy, who took his place, is also Catholic, but has upheld *Roe v. Wade*, to the bitter disappointment of antiabortion Catholics. Bork's conversion was a bittersweet victory: "With Bork on the court, *Roe* might have been overturned," one conservative Catholic activist suggested. "But on the court Bork might not have found God and the Church." In law, as in life, the shepherd sometimes abandons "the ninety-nine sheep to find the single lost one."

Scalia's career invites these sorts of reflections because he was outspoken about the Constitution and about Catholicism. When he spoke as a Catholic, he insisted that he wasn't speaking as a justice, and when he spoke as a justice, he insisted that his fidelity to the plain text of the Constitution insulated him from religious or ideological bias. Luckily for him, his Catholicism and his originalist conclusions generally happened to agree. Of course this was a fantasy: he was ideological in the extreme. Corey Robin devotes a chapter to Scalia in his study of *The Reactionary Mind*, and what emerges is a conservatism that "would have been recognizable to Social Darwinists of the late nineteenth century," and that manifested itself as a hostility to regulation, gun control, environmentalism, and the presidency of Al Gore. But Robin's greatest insight is about style: "Where others seek security" in their reading of the Constitution, "Scalia seeks sublimity." He relished the hard way, and saw "being tough and traditional" as "a heavy cross to bear." His excellent pun: "*Duresse oblige.*"

This, in a sense, is the convert's way. Scalia was a cradle Catholic, but as a jurist he wrote with the contrarian zeal, bite, and humor of a convert. Catholic converts, it is worth noting, have a curious position in modern intellectual history: the most important British and American intellectual voices of Catholicism, the historian Patrick Allitt notes, have been converts—John Henry Newman, G. K. Chesterton, Dorothy Day, Thomas Merton. This is not surprising, since the convert is best positioned to challenge former co-religionists and former coskeptics. The convert writes to convince or to annoy the as-yet-unconverted.

Scalia carried this energy into the secular arena of constitutional interpretation, and it could (or should) discomfit the Protestant as much as the secular humanist. He delighted in pointing out the heresies of his opponents. Ostentatious in his orthodoxy, he took pleasure in dogmatism for dogmatism's sake. Slippery-slope thinking is built into jurisprudence, but Scalia reveled in it especially, as the master of disproportionate outrage—hence the slope from homosexuality to murder, polygamy, and animal cruelty in *Romer v. Evans* (1996). He preferred the German term *Kulturkampf* to "culture war," as if the movement for gay rights were as powerful as Otto von Bismarck's campaign against Catholics in the 1870s. When, in

2001, the court let a disabled golfer ride in a cart during professional competition, in a case about the Americans with Disabilities Act, Scalia launched into a splenetic invocation of *Animal Farm*.

Eventually, convert intellectuals find themselves in peril, for what happens when the rock shifts beneath your feet? This brings us back to the pope's visit to Congress, and the absence of three of the court's Catholic conservatives: Samuel Alito, Thomas, and Scalia. Alito and Thomas had other engagements, apparently. Scalia's absence was more conspicuous, although he liked skipping congressional events, notably the State of the Union. Or maybe, with his disdain for international law, Scalia considered Francis's visit to be as irrelevant as the visit of any foreign head of state.

But the episode nevertheless draws attention to Scalia's disagreements with Rome, and it is grimly fitting to close with the sharpest of them: the morality and constitutionality of the death penalty. On this issue, Scalia's Catholicism and his originalism were most pronounced. (He noted with pleasure that Thomas More, who was himself beheaded in 1535, had no problem imposing the death penalty as Lord Chancellor of England.) The Vatican's opposition to the death penalty predates Pope Francis; John Paul II's encyclical *Evangelium Vitae* (1995) condemned it, along with abortion and euthanasia. Scalia could follow the pope's position on abortion and euthanasia, but not on the death penalty. In a 2002 speech at the University of Chicago Divinity School, published in *First Things*, Scalia held to the harder line, noting that "the more Christian a country is, the *less* likely it is to regard the death penalty as immoral." How else to account for the fact that "post-Christian Europe" was where the death-penalty-abolition movement was most successful, while support for the death penalty is still strong in the "church-going United States"? In a line that has often been taken out of context, his explanation was that "for the believing Christian, death is no big deal."

What he meant was that as a moral matter, the death penalty seems horrible only if you believe that execution ends someone's existence; if execution sends that person to God, then it *can* (though might not always) be just. The church had been tricked, or was betraying itself: the modern Vatican's "opposition to the death penalty is the legacy of Napoleon, Hegel, and Freud rather than St. Paul and St. Augustine." As a constitutional matter, it was absurd to suggest that the death penalty violates the Eighth Amendment, because none of the framers who put "cruel and unusual" into the Constitution thought the death penalty was cruel and unusual. To ignore that was like Jefferson ignoring the resurrection. This was a classic Scalia line of argument: erudite, logically convincing, but dogmatic in a way that makes it fruitless to argue with. It is like arguing with a piece of cake.

Much has and will be written about Scalia's legacy, and about whether originalism will carry on without him. He made the liberals on the bench bicker about the 18th century, which was at least a victory for antiquarians. But liberal originalisms have emerged to co-opt Scalia's conservative variety, and even the conservatives sometimes mocked his logic, as when Alito snarkily wondered whether Scalia wanted to know "what James Madison thought about video games." (Scalia, cleverer than Alito, replied, "No, I want to know what James Madison thought about violence," a statement behind which I like to infer an original intent to punch Alito in the mouth.) I am left wondering how useful or worthy he was as an

opponent; whether his conservatism had the effect of strengthening liberalism. He was often a terrible ally, and wrote few majority opinions because his arguments were too extreme to convince a moderate. But his ideological opponents on the court reportedly looked forward to his blistering comments, which toughened their own thinking. That may be his most lasting contribution, and it makes sense, for his originalism is a contrarian's creed. It exists primarily to disagree, and it reaches its apotheosis in dissent.

By now it's a commonplace that Scalia had a "brilliant legal mind," but eventually the habits of recalcitrance, absolutism, and scorn disqualify a mind from brilliance. And a hermetic disregard for the real suffering of people eventually qualifies as a sin, however gloriously that sin is cloaked in originalism, textualism, traditionalism, anti-purposivism, or "judicial restraint." For instance, Scalia's interpretation of "the right of the people to keep and bear arms" was flatly wrong, even by his own yardstick of fidelity to the historical meaning of the Constitution, and cruel in its amorality. In general, Scalia's influence was a scourge visited on democracy. In that sense, at least, his originalism was grounded in history, for the original Constitution was in many ways an undemocratic document. It put the election of the President in the hands of an arcane electoral college, and it pointedly gave no say to the House of Representatives, our only directly elected governing body, in the selection of Supreme Court justices. Scalia's originalism was bound inescapably to the values of the propertied, often slave-owning, white men who authored this Constitution. But that need not be the original vision we are stuck with, because even in 1787, "We the People" meant more than Scalia wanted it to mean. +

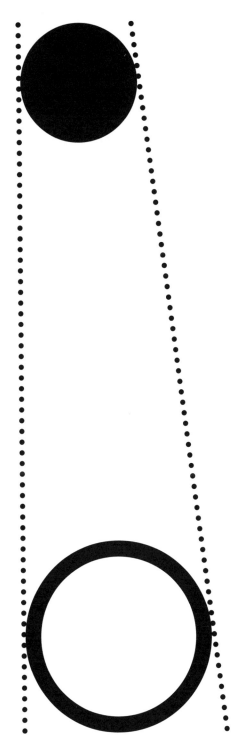

ESMERINE
Lost Voices

OUGHT
Sun Coming Down

JERUSALEM IN MY HEART
If He Dies, If If If If If If

MATANA ROBERTS
Coin Coin Chapter Three:
river run thee

**COLIN STETSON
AND SARAH NEUFELD**
Never were the way she was

**AVEC LE SOLEIL
SORTANT DE SA BOUCHE**
Zubberdust!

**GODSPEED YOU!
BLACK EMPEROR**
'Asunder, Sweet And
Other Distress'

ERIC CHENAUX
Skullsplitter

SISKIYOU
Nervous

LAST EX
Last Ex

All titles on Deluxe 180gLP • CD • MP3 • FLAC

CONSTELLATION cstrecords.com

McNALLY JACKSON

✦

To understand a profound thought is to have, at the moment one understands it, a profound thought oneself; and this demands some effort, a genuine descent to the heart of oneself.
—MARCEL PROUST

INDEPENDENT BOOKSELLERS

52 PRINCE STREET IN NOLITA

MCNALLYJACKSON.COM

EST. 2004

JENNIFER MURPHY, *GOLD AND BLACK CIRCLES*. 2007, GOLD LEAF AND VELVET ON PAPER.
COURTESY CLINT ROENISCH GALLERY.

UNCANNY VALLEY

Anna Wiener

ORALE IS DOWN. We are making plenty of money, but the office
is teeming with salespeople: well-groomed social animals with
good posture and dress shoes, men who chuckle and smooth their hair
back when they can't connect to our VPN. Their corner of the office is
loud; their desks are scattered with freebies from other start-ups, stick-
ers and koozies and flash drives. We escape for drinks and fret about
our company culture. "Our culture is dying," we say gravely, apocalyptic
prophets all. "What should we do about the culture?"

It's not just the salespeople, of course. It's never just the salespeople.
Our culture has been splintering for months. Members of our core team
have been shepherded into conference rooms by top-level executives
who proceed to question our loyalty. They've noticed the sea change.
They've noticed we don't seem as invested. We don't stick around for
in-office happy hour anymore; we don't take new hires out for lunch on
the company card. We're not hitting our KPIs, we're not serious about
the OKRs. People keep using the word *paranoid*. Our primary investor
has funded a direct competitor. This is what investors do, but it feels
personal: Daddy still loves us, but he loves us less.

We get ourselves out of the office and into a bar. We have more in
common than our grievances, but we kick off by speculating about our
job security, complaining about the bureaucratic double-downs, casting blame for blocks and poor product decisions. We talk about our
IPO like it's the deus ex machina coming down from on high to save
us—like it's an inevitability, like our stock options will lift us out of our
existential dread, away from the collective anxiety that ebbs and flows.

Realistically, we know it could be years before an IPO, if there's an IPO at all; we know in our hearts that money is a salve, not a solution. Still, we are hopeful. We reassure ourselves and one another that this is just a phase; every start-up has its growing pains. Eventually we are drunk enough to change the subject, to remember our more private selves. The people we are on weekends, the people we were for years.

This is a group of secret smokers, and we go in on a communal pack of cigarettes. The problem, we admit between drags, is that we *do* care. We care about one another. We even care about the executives who can make us feel like shit. We want good lives for them, just like we want good lives for ourselves. We care, for fuck's sake, about the company culture. We are among the first twenty employees, and we are making something people want. It feels like ours. Work has wedged its way into our identities, and the only way to maintain sanity is to maintain that we are the company, the company is us. Whenever we see a stranger at the gym wearing a T-shirt with our logo on it, whenever we are mentioned on social media or on a client's blog, whenever we get a positive support ticket, we share it in the company chat room and we're proud, genuinely proud.

But we see now that we've been swimming in the Kool-Aid, and we're coming up for air. We were lucky and in thrall and now we are bureaucrats, punching at our computers, making other people—some *kids*—unfathomably rich. We throw our dead cigarettes on the sidewalk and grind them out under our toes. Phones are opened and taxis summoned; we gulp the dregs of our beers as cartoon cars approach on-screen. We disperse, off to terrorize sleeping roommates and lovers, to answer just one, two more emails before bed. Eight hours later we'll be back in the office, slurping down coffee, running out for congealed breakfast sandwiches, tweaking mediocre scripts and writing half-hearted emails, throwing weary and knowing glances across the table.

I SKIM RECRUITER EMAILS and job listings like horoscopes, skidding down to the perks: competitive salary, dental and vision, 401k, free gym membership, catered lunch, bike storage, ski trips to Tahoe, offsites to Napa, summits in Vegas, beer on tap, craft beer on tap, kombucha on tap, wine tastings, Whiskey Wednesdays, Open Bar Fridays, massage on-site, yoga on-site, pool table, Ping-Pong table, Ping-Pong robot, ball pit, game night, movie night, go-karts, zip line. Job listings are an excellent place to get sprayed with HR's idea of fun and a 23-year-old's idea of work-life balance. Sometimes I forget I'm not applying to summer camp. *Customized setup: design your ultimate work station with the latest hardware. Change the world around you. Help humanity thrive by enabling*—next! *We work hard, we laugh hard, we give great high-fives. We have engineers in TopCoder's Top 20. We're not just another social web app. We're not just another project-management tool. We're not just another payment processor.* I get a haircut and start exploring.

Most start-up offices look the same—faux midcentury furniture, brick walls, snack bar, bar cart. Interior designers in Silicon Valley are either brand-conscious or very literal. When tech products are projected into the physical world they become aesthetics unto themselves, as if to insist on their own reality: the office belonging to a home-sharing website is decorated like rooms in its customers' pool houses and pieds-à-terre; the foyer of a hotel-booking start-up has a concierge desk replete with bell (no concierge); the headquarters of a ride-sharing app gleams in the same colors as the app itself, down to the sleek elevator bank. A book-related start-up holds a small and sad library, the shelves half-empty, paperbacks and object-oriented-programming manuals sloping against one another. It reminds me of the people who dressed like Michael Jackson to attend Michael Jackson's funeral.

But this office, of a media app with millions in VC funding but no revenue model, is particularly sexy. This is something that an office shouldn't be, and it jerks my heart rate way, way up. There are views of the city in every direction, fat leather loveseats, electric guitars plugged into amps, teak credenzas with white hardware. It looks like the loft apartment of the famous musician boyfriend I thought I'd have at 22 but somehow never met. I want to take off my dress and my shoes and lie on the voluminous sheepskin rug and eat fistfuls of MDMA, curl my naked body into the Eero Aarnio Ball Chair, never leave.

It's not clear whether I'm here for lunch or an interview, which is normal. I am prepared for both and dressed for neither. My guide leads me through the communal kitchen, which has the trappings of every other start-up pantry: plastic bins of trail mix and Goldfish, bowls of Popchips and miniature candy bars. There's the requisite wholesale box of assorted Clif Bars, and in the fridge are flavored water, string cheese, and single-serving cartons of chocolate milk. It can be hard to tell whether a company is training for a marathon or eating an after-school snack. Once I walked into our kitchen and found two Account Managers pounding Shot Bloks, chewy cubes of glucose marketed to endurance athletes.

Over catered Afghan food, I meet the team, including a billionaire who made his fortune from a website that helps people feel close to celebrities and other strangers they'd hate in real life. He asks where I work, and I tell him. "Oh," he says, not unkindly, snapping a piece of lavash in two, "I know that company. I think I tried to buy you."

I TAKE ANOTHER PERSONAL DAY without giving a reason, an act of defiance that I fear is transparent. I spend the morning drinking coffee and skimming breathless tech press, then creep downtown to spend the afternoon in back-to-back interviews at a peanut-size start-up. All of the interviews are with men, which is fine. I like men. I had a boyfriend; I have a brother. The men ask me questions like, "How would you calculate the number of people who work for the United States Postal Service?" and "How would you describe the internet to a medieval farmer?" and "What is the hardest thing you've ever done?" They tell me to stand in front of the whiteboard and diagram my responses. These questions are self-conscious and infuriating, but it only serves to fuel me. I want to impress; I refuse to be discouraged by their self-importance. Here is a character flaw, my industry origin story: I have always responded positively to negging.

My third interview is with the technical cofounder. He enters the conference room in a crisp blue button-down, looking confidently unprepared. He tells me—apologetically—that he hasn't done many interviews before, and as such he doesn't have a ton of questions to ask me. Nonetheless, the office manager slated an hour for our conversation. This seems OK: I figure we will talk about the company, I will ask routine follow-up questions, and at four they will let me out for the day, like a middle school student, and the city will absorb me and my private errors. Then he tells me that his girlfriend is applying to law school and he's been helping her prep. So instead of a conventional interview, he's just going to have me take a section of the LSAT. I search his face to see if he's kidding.

"If it's cool with you, I'm just going to hang out here and check my email," he says, sliding the test across the table and opening a laptop. He sets a timer.

I finish early, ever the overachiever. I check it twice. The cofounder grades it on the spot. "My mother would be so proud," I joke, feeling brilliant and misplaced and low, lower than low.

H OME IS MY REFUGE, except when it's not. My roommate is turning 30, and to celebrate we are hosting a wine and cheese party at our apartment. Well, she is hosting—I have been invited. Her friends arrive promptly, in business casual. Hundreds of dollars of cheese are represented. "Bi-Rite, obviously," she says, looking elegant in black silk as she smears Humboldt Fog onto a cracker. My roommate works down on the Peninsula, for a website that everyone loathes but no one can stop using. We occupy different spaces: I am in the start-up world, land of perpetual youth, and she is an adult like any other, navigating a corporation, acting the part, negotiating for her place. I admire and do not understand her; it is possible she finds me amusing. Mostly we talk about exercise.

Classical music streams through the house and someone opens a bottle of proper Champagne, which he reassures us is really from France; people clap when the cork pops. My roommate and I are the same age but I feel like a child at my parents' party, and I am immediately envious, homesick. I send myself to my room, lock the door, and change into a very tight dress. I've gained fifteen pounds in trail mix: it never feels like a meal, but there's an aggregate effect. When I reenter the living room, I suck in my stomach and slide between people's backs, looking for a conversation. On the couch, a man in a suit jacket expounds on the cannabis opportunity. Everyone seems very comfortable and nobody talks to me. They tilt their wineglasses at the correct angle; they dust crumbs off their palms with grace. The word I hear the most is *revenue*. No—*strategy*. There's nothing to do but drink and ingratiate myself. I wind up on the roof with a cluster of strangers and find myself missing my mother with a ferocity that carves into my gut. In the distance I can see the tip of the famous Rainbow Flag on Castro Street, whipping.

"Oakland," one of them says. "That's where we want to invest."

"Too dangerous," says another. "My wife would never go for it."

"Of course not," says the first, "but you don't buy to *live* there."

By the time the last guest has filtered out, I am in leggings and a sweatshirt, cleaning ineffectively: scooping up cheese rinds, rinsing plastic glasses, sneaking slices of chocolate cake with my damp hands. My roommate comes to say goodnight, and she is beautiful: tipsy but not toasted, radiant with absorbed goodwill. She repairs to her room with her boyfriend, and I listen from down the hall as they quietly undress, ease into bed, turn over into sleep.

OURS IS A "PICKAX-DURING-THE-GOLD-RUSH" PRODUCT, the kind venture capitalists love to get behind. The product provides a shortcut to database infrastructure, giving people information about their apps and websites that they wouldn't necessarily have on their own. All our customers are other software companies. This is a privileged vantage point from which to observe the tech industry. I would say more, but I signed an NDA.

I am the inaugural customer support rep, or Support Engineer. My job involves looking at strangers' codebases and telling them what they've done wrong in integrating our product with theirs, and how to fix it. There are no unsolvable problems. Perhaps there are not even problems, only mistakes. After nearly three years in book publishing, where I mostly moved on instinct, taste, and feeling, the clarity of this soothes me.

I learn the bare minimum, code-wise, to be able to do my job well—to ask questions only when I'm truly in over my head. Still, I escalate problems all the time. I learn how to talk to our customers about the technology without ever touching the technology itself. I find myself confidently discussing cookies, data mapping, the difference between server-side and client-side integrations. "Just add logic!" I advise cheerfully. This means nothing to me but generally resonates with engineers. It shocks me every time someone nods along.

This is not to confuse confidence with pride. I doubt myself daily. I feel lucky to have this job; I feel desperately out of place. My previous boss—breezy and helpful, earnest in the manner of a man in his early twenties bequeathed $4 million to disrupt libraries—had encouraged me to apply for the role; I had joined his publishing start-up too early and needed something new. "This is the next big company," he had said. "It's a rocket ship." He was right. I had been banking on him being right. Still, there are days when all I want is to disembark, eject myself into space, admit defeat. I pander and apologize and self-deprecate until my manager criticizes me for being a pleaser, at which point it seems most strategic to stop talking.

I convince myself and everyone else that I want to learn how to code, and I'm incentivized to do it: I'm told I will be promoted to Solutions

Architect if I can build a networked, two-player game of checkers in the next few months. One lazy Saturday I give it three hours, then call it a day. I resent the challenge; I resent myself. I tell everyone I can't do it, which is a lesser evil than not wanting to. In this environment, my lack of interest in learning JavaScript feels like a moral failure.

Around here, we nonengineers are pressed to prove our value. The hierarchy is pervasive, ingrained in the industry's dismissal of marketing and its insistence that a good product sells itself; evident in the few "office hours" established for engineers (our scheduled opportunity to approach with questions and bugs); reflected in our salaries and equity allotment, even though it's harder to find a good copywriter than a liberal-arts graduate with a degree in history and twelve weeks' training from an uncredentialed coding dojo. This is a cozy home for believers in bootstrapping and meritocracy, proponents of shallow libertarianism. I am susceptible to it, too. "He just taught himself to code over the summer," I hear myself say one afternoon, with the awe of someone relaying a miracle.

Our soft skills are a necessary inconvenience. We bloat payroll; we dilute conversation; we create process and bureaucracy; we put in requests for yoga classes and Human Resources. We're a dragnet—though we tend to contribute positively to diversity metrics. There is quiet pity for the MBAs.

It's easy for me to dissociate from the inferiority of my job because I've never been particularly proud of my customer-service skills. I'm good at subservience, but it isn't what I would lead with on a first date. I enjoy translating between the software and the customers. I like breaking down information, demystifying technical processes, being one of few with this specific expertise. I like being bossy. People are interesting—unpredictable, emotional—when their expensive software product doesn't behave as expected. Plus, I am almost always permissioned for God Mode.

After a year, my job evolves from support into something the industry calls Customer Success. The new role is more interesting, but the title is so corny and oddly stilted in its pseudosincerity that I cannot bring myself to say it out loud. This turns out to work to my advantage: when I change my email signature to read "Technical Account Manager" instead, it actually elicits a response from previously uncommunicative clients who are—I regret having to buttress stereotypes—always engineers, always founders, and always men.

I visit a friend at his midsize software company and see a woman typing at a treadmill desk. *That's a little on the nose*, I whisper, and he whispers back, *You have no idea—she does Customer Success.*

M Y COWORKERS ARE ALL SKILLED at maneuvering something called a RipStik, a two-wheeled, skateboard-like invention with separated pivoting plates, one for each foot. They glide across the office, twisting and dipping with laptops in hand, taking customer calls on their personal cell phones, shuttling from desk to kitchen to conference room. Mastering the RipStik is a rite of passage, and I cannot do it. After a few weeks of trying, I order a tiny plastic skateboard off eBay, a neon-green Penny board with four wheels that looks coolest when it's not being ridden. I come into the office over the weekend and practice on the Penny, perfecting my balance. It's fast, dangerously so. Mostly I put it under my standing desk and then get onboard, rocking back and forth as I work.

T HE BILLBOARDS ALONG THE STRETCH of the 101 that sweeps Silicon Valley have been punchy and declarative lately, advertising apps and other software products that transcend all context and grammatical structure. "We fixed dinner" (meal delivery). "Ask your developer" (cloud-based communications). "How tomorrow works" (file storage). The ads get less dystopian the farther you get from the city: by the airport, they grow international-businessman corporate, and as the land turns over into suburbs you can almost hear the gears shift. A financial-services company—one that's been around for more than a century, a provider of life insurance, investment management, and, in the 1980s, bald-faced fraud—holds a mirror to an audience that perhaps won't want to recognize itself. The ad reads, "Donate to a worthy cause: your retirement."

I attend a networking event at an office whose walls are hung with inspirational posters that quote tech luminaries I've never heard of. The posters say things like "Life is short: build stuff that matters" and "Innovate or die." I am dead. Our interior designer tried hanging posters like these in our office; the front-end engineers relocated them to the bathroom, placed them face to the wall. The event is packed; people roam in clusters, like college freshmen during orientation week. There are a few women, but most of the attendees are young men in start-up twinsets: I pass someone wearing a branded hoodie, unzipped to reveal a shirt with the same logo. I google the company on my cellphone to see what it is, to see if they're hiring. "We have loved mobile since we saw Steve Jobs announce the first iPhone," their website declares, and I close the browser, thinking, *how basic.*

The tenor of these events is usually the same: guilelessly optimistic. People are excited to talk about their start-ups, and all small-talk is a prelude to a pitch. I'm guilty of this, too; I'm proud of my work, and our recruiting bonus is 15 percent of my salary (alignment of company–employee goals and incentives). I talk to two European men who are building a food-delivery app geared toward healthy eaters, like people on the Paleo diet. They're extremely polite and oddly buff. They say they'll invite me to their beta, and I am excited. I like to be on the inside track. I want to help. I tell them that I know a lot of people on the Paleo diet, like the guy in marketing who stores plastic baggies of wet, sauteed meat in the communal refrigerator. I chatter on about Paleo adherents and people who do CrossFit and practice polyamory, and how I admire that they manage to do these things without detrimental physical or emotional consequences. I've learned so much about polyamory and S&M since moving to San Francisco. Ask me anything about *The Ethical Slut*; ask me anything about *Sex at Dawn.* That night, I download the healthy-food app and can't ever imagine using it.

My opinion doesn't matter, of course: a few months later I'll find out that the Europeans raised $30-odd million after pivoting to a new business model and undergoing a radical rebranding, and I'll find this out when our company starts paying them thousands to organize the catering for our in-office meals. The food is served in sturdy tinfoil troughs, and people race to be first in line for self-serve. It is low-carb and delicious, healthier than anything I've ever cooked, well worth someone else's money, and every afternoon I shovel it into my body.

OUR OWN 101 BILLBOARD is unveiled on a chilly morning in November, just a few months after I've started. Everyone gets to work early; our office manager orders fresh-squeezed orange juice and pastries, cups of yogurt parfait with granola strata. We've arranged for a company field trip around the corner. We walk in a pack, hands in our pockets, and take a group photograph in front of our ad. I forward it to my parents in New York. In the photograph we've got our arms around one another, smiling and proud. The start-up is still small, just thirty of us or so, but within a year we'll be almost a hundred employees, and shortly thereafter, I'll be gone.

I HAVE LUNCH with one of the salespeople, and I like him a lot. He's easy to talk to; he's easy to talk to for a living. We eat large, sloppy sandwiches in the park and gaze out at the tourists.

"So how'd you end up choosing our company?" I ask. Roast turkey drops from my sandwich onto the grass.

"Come on," he says. "I heard there were a bunch of twentysome-things crushing it in the Valley. How often does that happen?"

I lean in and go to a panel on big data. There are two venture capitalists onstage, dressed identically. They are exceptionally sweaty. Even from the back row, the place feels moist. I've never been in a room with so few women and so much money, and so many people champing at the bit to get a taste. It's like watching two ATMs in conversation. "I want big data on men watching other men talk about data," I whisper to my new friend in sales, who ignores me.

Back at the office, I walk into the bathroom to find a coworker folded over the sink, wiping her face with a paper towel. There aren't many women at this company, and I have encountered almost all of them, at one point or another, crying in the bathroom. "I just hope this is all worth it," she spits in my direction. I know what she means—she's talking about money—but I also know how much equity she has, and I'm confident that even in the best possible scenario, whatever she's experiencing is definitely not. She's out the door and back at her desk before I can conjure up something consoling.

Half of the conversations I overhear these days are about money, but nobody likes to get specific. It behooves everyone to stay theoretical.

A friend's roommate wins a hackathon with corporate sponsorship, and on a rainy Sunday afternoon he is awarded $500,000. (It is actually a million, but who would believe me?) That evening they throw a party at their duplex, which feels like a normal event in the Burning Man off-season—whippits, face paint, high-design vaporizers—except for the over-size foamcore check propped laterally against the bathroom doorframe.

Out by the porch cooler, I run into a friend who works at a company—cloud something—that was recently acquired. I make a joke about this being a billionaire boys' club and he laughs horsily, disproportionate to the humor. I've never seen him like this, but then I've never met anyone who's won the lottery, seen anyone so jazzed on his own good luck. He opens a beer using the edge of his lighter and invites me to drive up to Mendocino in his new convertible. What else do you do after a windfall? "You know who the real winner was, though?" he asks, then immediately names a mutual acquaintance, a brilliant and introverted programmer who was the company's first engineering hire, very likely the linchpin. "Instant multimillionaire," my friend says incredulously, as if hearing his own information for the first time. "At least eight figures."

"Wow," I say, handing my beer to him to open. "What do you think he wants to do?"

My friend deftly pops off the bottle cap, then looks at me and shrugs. "That's a good question," he says, tapping the lighter against the side of his beer. "I don't think he wants to do anything."

AN OLD HIGH SCHOOL FRIEND emails out of the blue to introduce me to his college buddy: a developer, new to the city, "always a great time!" The developer and I agree to meet for drinks. It's not clear whether we're meeting for a date or networking. Not that there's always a difference: I have one friend who found a job by swiping right and know countless others who go to industry conferences just to fuck—nothing gets them hard like a nonsmoking room charged to the company AmEx. The developer is very handsome and stiltedly sweet. He seems like someone who has opinions about fonts, and he does. It's clear from the start that we're there to talk shop. We go to a tiny cocktail bar in the Tenderloin with textured wallpaper and a scrawny bouncer. Photographs are forbidden, which means the place is designed for social media. This city is changing, and I am disgusted by my own complicity.

"There's no menu, so you can't just order, you know, a martini," the developer says, as if I would ever. "You tell the bartender three adjectives, and he'll customize a drink for you accordingly. It's great. It's creative! I've been thinking about my adjectives all day."

What is it like to be fun? What is it like to feel like you've earned this? I try to game the system by asking for something smoky, salty, and angry, crossing my fingers for mezcal; it works. We lean against a wall and sip. The developer tells me about his loft apartment in the Mission, his specialty bikes, how excited he is to go on weeknight camping trips. We talk about cameras and books. We talk about cities we've never visited. I tell him about the personal-shopper service my coworkers all signed up for, how three guys came into work wearing the same sweater; he laughs but looks a little guilty. He's sweet and a little shy about his intelligence, and I know we'll probably never hang out again. Still, I go home that night with the feeling that something, however small, has been lifted.

VENTURE CAPITALISTS HAVE SPEARHEADED massive innovation in the past few decades, not least of which is their incubation of this generation's very worst prose style. The internet is choked with blindly ambitious and professionally inexperienced men giving each other anecdote-based instruction and bullet-point advice. *10 Essential Start-up Lessons You Won't Learn in School. 10 Things Every Successful Entrepreneur Knows. 5 Ways to Stay Humble. Why the Market Always Wins. Why the Customer Is Never Right. How to Deal with Failure. How to Fail Better. How to Fail Up. How to Pivot. How to Pivot Back. 18 Platitudes to Tape Above Your Computer. Raise Your Way to Emotional Acuity. How to Love Something That Doesn't Love You Back.*

Sometimes it feels like everyone is speaking a different language—or the same language, with radically different rules. At our all-hands meeting, we are subjected to a pep talk. Our director looks like he hasn't slept in days, but he straightens up and moves his gaze from face to face, making direct and metered eye contact with everyone around the table. "We are making products," he begins, "that can push the fold of mankind."

A networking-addicted coworker scrolls through a website where people voluntarily post their own résumés. I spy. He clicks through to an engineer who works for an aggressively powerful start-up, one whose rapid expansion, relentless pursuit of domination, and absence of ethical boundaries scare the shit out of me. Under his current company, the engineer has written this job description: "This is a rocket ship, baby. Climb aboard."

I am waiting for the train when I notice the ad: it covers the platform below the escalators. The product is an identity-as-a-service app—it stores passwords—but the company isn't advertising to users; they're advertising their job openings. They're advertising to me. The ad features five people standing in V-formation with their arms crossed.

They're all wearing identical blue hoodies. They're also wearing identical rubber unicorn masks; I am standing on one of their heads. The copy reads, "Built by humans, used by unicorns."

W E HIRE AN ENGINEER fresh out of a top undergraduate program. She walks confidently into the office, springy and enthusiastic. We've all been looking forward to having a woman on our engineering team. It's a big moment for us. Her onboarding buddy brings her around to make introductions, and as they approach our corner, my coworker leans over and cups his hand around my ear: as though we are colluding, as though we are 5 years old. "I feel sorry," he says, his breath moist against my neck. "Everyone's going to hit on her."

I include this anecdote in an email to my mom. The annual-review cycle is nigh, and I'm on the fence about whether or not to bring up the running list of casual hostilities toward women that add unsolicited spice to the workplace. I tell her about the colleague with the smart-watch app that's just an animated GIF of a woman's breasts bouncing in perpetuity; I tell her about the comments I've fielded about my weight, my lips, my clothing, my sex life; I tell her that the first woman engineer is also the only engineer without SSH access to the servers. I tell her that compared with other women I've met here, I have it good, but the bar is low. It's tricky: I like these coworkers—and I dish it back—but in the parlance of our industry, this behavior is scalable. I don't have any horror stories yet; I'd prefer things stay this way. I expect my mother to respond with words of support and encouragement. I expect her to say, "Yes! You are the change this industry needs." She emails me back almost immediately. "Don't put complaints about sexism in writing," she writes. "Unless, of course, you have a lawyer at the ready."

A MEETING IS DROPPED MYSTERIOUSLY onto our calendars, and at the designated time we shuffle warily into a conference room. The last time this happened, we were given forms that asked us to rate various values on a scale of 1 to 5: our desire to lead a team; the importance of work-life balance. I gave both things a 4 and was told I didn't want it enough.

The conference room has a million-dollar view of downtown San Francisco, but we keep the shades down. Across the street, a bucket drummer bangs out an irregular heartbeat. We sit in a row, backs to the window, laptops open. I look around the room and feel a wave of affection for these men, this small group of misfits who are the only people who understand this new backbone to my life. On the other side of the table, our manager paces back and forth, but he's smiling. He asks us to write down the names of the five smartest people we know, and we dutifully oblige. I look at the list and think about how much I miss my friends back home, how bad I've been at returning phone calls and emails, how bloated I've become with start-up self-importance, how I've stopped making time for what I once held dear. I can feel blood rush to my cheeks.

"OK," my manager says. "Now tell me: why don't they work here?"

M ORALE, LIKE ANYTHING, is just another problem to be solved. There is a high premium on break/fix. To solve our problem, management arranges for a team-building exercise. They schedule it on a week-night evening, and we pretend not to mind. Our team-building begins with beers in the office, and then we travel en masse to a tiny event space at the mouth of the Stockton Tunnel, where two energetic blondes give us sweatbands and shots. The blondes are attractive and athletic, strong limbs wrapped in spandex leggings and tiny shorts, and we are their smudge-edged foils: an army of soft bellies and stiff necks, hands tight with the threat of carpal tunnel. They smear neon face paint across our foreheads and cheeks and tell us we look awesome. The event space warms up as people get drunk and bounce around the room, taking selfies with the CFO, fist-bumping the cofounders without irony, flirting with the new hires who don't yet know any better. We play Skee-Ball. We cluster by the bar and have another round, two.

Eventually, we're dispatched on a scavenger hunt across the city. We pour out of the building and into the street, spreading across rush-hour San Francisco, seeking landmarks; we barrel past tourists and harass taxicab drivers, piss off doormen and stumble into homeless people. We are our own worst representatives, calling apologies over our shoulders. We are sweaty, competitive—maybe happy, really happy.

T HE MEETING BEGINS without fanfare. They thought I was an amazing worker at first, working late every night, last out of the office, but now they wonder if the work was just too hard for me to begin with. They need to know: Am I down for the cause? Because if I'm not down for the cause, it's time. They will do this amicably. Of course I'm down,

I say, trying not to swivel in my ergonomic chair. I care deeply about the company. I am here for it.

When I say I care deeply, what I mean is I am ready to retire. When I say I'm down, what I mean is I'm scared. I cry twice during the meeting, despite my best efforts. I think about the city I left to come here, the plans I've canceled and the friends I haven't made. I think about how hard I've worked and how demoralizing it is to fail. I think about my values, and I cry even more. It will be months until I call uncle and quit; it will take almost a year to realize I was gaslighting myself, that I was reading from someone else's script.

IT'S CHRISTMASTIME; I'm older, I'm elsewhere. On the train to work, I swipe through social media and hit on a post from the start-up's holiday party, which has its own hashtag. The photograph is of two former teammates, both of them smiling broadly, their teeth as white as I remember. "So grateful to be part of such an amazing team," the caption reads, and I tap through. The hashtag unleashes a stream of photographs featuring people I've never met—beautiful people, the kind of people who look good in athleisure. They look well rested. They look relaxed and happy. They look nothing like me. There's a photograph of what can only be the pre-dinner floor show: an acrobat in a leotard kneeling on a pedestal, her legs contorted, her feet grasping a bow and arrow, poised to release. Her target is a stuffed heart, printed with the company logo. I scroll past animated photo-booth GIFs of strangers, kissing and mugging for the camera, and I recognize their pride, I empathize with their sense of accomplishment—this was one hell of a year, and they have won. I feel gently ill, a callback to the childhood nausea of being left out.

The holiday party my year at the company began with an open bar at 4 PM—the same coworker had shellacked my hair into curls in the office bathroom, both of us excited and exhausted, ready to celebrate. Hours later, we danced against the glass windows of the *Michelin*-starred restaurant our company had bought out for the night, our napkins strewn on the tables, our shoes torn off, our plus-ones shifting in formal wear on the sidelines, the waitstaff studiously withholding visible judgment.

I keep scrolling until I hit a video of this year's after-party, which looks like it was filmed in a club or at a flashy bar mitzvah, save for the company logo projected onto the wall: flashing colored lights illuminate men in stripped-down suits and women in cocktail dresses, all of them bouncing up and down, waving glow sticks and lightsabers to a background of electronic dance music. They've gone pro, I say to myself. "Last night was epic!" someone has commented. Three years have passed since I left. I catch myself searching for my own face anyway. +

printtext.co | A periodicals shop, studio & project space | @printtext

WHITNEY HUBBS, *UNTITLED*. COURTESY THE ARTIST.

BURN SCARS

Philip Connors

Like any Romantic, I had always been vaguely certain that sometime during my life I should come into a magic place which in disclosing its secrets would give me wisdom and ecstasy—perhaps even death.

—Paul Bowles

Infrared waves just below twenty hertz associated with approaching thunder seem to have strange effects on the temporal lobe in some part of the population, to wit producing feelings of baseless awe and ecstasy.

—Norman Rush

I THOUGHT I HEARD A SHOUT from far below. Snug in the cocoon of my sleeping bag, face averted from the honey-colored sunrise pouring through the windows, I could not at first remember where I was and why. For a moment I experienced the tingly, dissociative terror one feels on waking from a bad dream—only to realize I was waking into one.

The shout came twice more before I recognized the voice and hollered back. It belonged to Teresa, fiancée of my friend John, whom we had both been mourning for three weeks. She had started up the mountain on foot before daybreak, a steep two and a half miles from the trailhead. Sleep eluded her past about three in the morning, so she found ways to make use of the dawn hours, fueled by plenty of coffee. For me the trouble was the night, but I stumbled through with the time-tested crutch of whiskey, neat.

During a dozen summers of lookout duty I had mostly spent my nights in a cabin at ground level, in another mountain range entirely, but there was no cabin on John's peak, only the tower—a spacious live-in model. I invited Teresa up the stairs, feeling almost embarrassed at having to proffer an invitation. She had spent far more time there than I had, hanging out with John; I was merely an emergency fill-in, on loan from a different ranger district twenty miles east. A fire there the previous summer had left my home tower surrounded by a 214-square-mile burn scar: a bird's nest marooned in a charscape. There wasn't a whole lot left to catch fire in that country, so my boss figured he could spare me for a few weeks while I covered John's shifts on Signal Peak, and my relief lookout worked extra to cover mine.

I slipped into my pants and donned a hat while Teresa's hiking boots rang on the tower's metal steps. Given her intimate understanding of the profession, she refused to climb an occupied lookout without permission from its resident caretaker, a recognition that fire towers serve not merely as scenic overlooks for tourists but as actual work spaces for lookouts, some of whom consider pants optional.

Rare is the pleasure hiker whose appreciation of the wild is capacious enough to include a surprise confrontation with a hairy human ass. Nonetheless, an unsettling number of visitors disregarded the sign at the base of the tower informing the curious that the structure had an official purpose, and that permission was required to climb it during its annual period of occupancy, roughly April through August. People being people, a few began their thoughtless trudge up the stairs without even a hollered warning. Maybe this impertinence had something to do with the implausibility, in our day and age, of someone still getting paid to stare out the window at mountains all day; maybe certain humans could no longer be bothered to read from a surface other than a screen. In any case, when John had ruled the roost he would tweak trespassers by meeting them partway in their ascent and telling them he was in the middle of some very important paperwork, and if they would wait at the base of the tower for ten or fifteen minutes—twenty tops—he would have the *I*s dotted and the *T*s crossed and be glad to share the view. Then he would return to his glass-walled perch on stilts and laugh to himself. The fact that there was no paperwork was part of what we loved about the job.

I joined Teresa on the catwalk. We stood against the railing looking north toward the big mountains, where tinsel tufts of cloud hovered over the creases in the land, the canyons and the river valleys. It was one of those mornings of fresh-scrubbed serenity that made the forest look like a world at the dawn of time—a view so magnanimous with earthly beauty it made me want to live forever, even as I was more aware than usual that I would not.

Although her days as a freak on a peak were behind her, Teresa still surpassed me by almost two decades of experience in the lookout's game, having worked thirty seasons in total, most of them on two mountains—Black Mountain, Bearwallow—in our shared home forest, the Gila of southern New Mexico. She last occupied Bearwallow the year before I showed up on the Gila; my first season coincided with her venturing north to work towers in Oregon and Idaho, so I had missed out on the pleasure of hearing her voice on the two-way radio. Hearing it now, in person, I felt sadness and gratitude at once; the sadness would have been there either way, with or without her presence, but I was grateful I wouldn't feel compelled to hide it from her, as I would have from the average day hiker—that on the contrary I could share it with her, and share in hers. Perhaps in this way we could soften it for each other just a little.

In the distance we could see the Gila Wilderness, the original American experiment in protecting wild country from incursion by industrial machines. In 1924, as an idealistic young forester, Aldo Leopold had convinced his superiors in the Forest Service to draw a jagged boundary line around the only mountains left in the American Southwest not carved up by roads and keep them that way. His plan made the Gila the world's first Wilderness with a capital *W*, meaning no automobiles, no tourist developments of any kind, all travel demanding the exertions of animate flesh, either one's own or that of a horse: the model for what would become, forty years later, the Wilderness Act. True to Leopold's vision, this exercise in willed restraint had preserved, for ninety years and running, a big enough stretch of country to allow for packing with mules on a trip lasting two weeks during which the pack string never once crossed its own tracks. Even if he weren't venerated as the high priest of American ecology, having forever changed the way we think about the natural world thanks to his visionary land ethic, Leopold would be remembered for changing our relationship with some pretty big chunks of it—none more resonant with symbolism than the Gila. For some of us it remained not only the first Wilderness but the best: more than half a million acres of grassland, mountain, and mesa, the major sky-island bridge between the southern Rockies and the northern Sierra Madre.

Teresa had seen more of that place than anyone I knew, and I never tired of hearing her stories of riding the trails with old-time mule packers, or floating the river's forks at flood stage in a battered boat. These were uncommon pursuits, to put it mildly. Packing with mules had always been so, and those who boated in that country ran the Gila River's main stem, not the smaller and gnarlier headwaters forks. Those forks were too small, offered too many challenges, involved too much boat-dragging and bushwhacking. I had never heard of anyone else attempting to float them. For Teresa, that was part of the allure: the difficulty, the novelty. That, and the occasion for solitude. Hers was an undomesticated sensibility of an especially intense kind, fueled by a passion for wild creatures and native flora, making for a life lived around ranchers and firefighters and others who worked outdoors, fuel-wood cutters and horse breeders and their ilk. She had more than held her own in that world. She was what was called an "old Gila hand"—*hand* being the most respectful moniker bestowed on humans in wild country, and *old* not an epithet but an honorific.

Her adventures had hardly been limited to the Gila. She had once run the Green River solo, from northern Utah to Lake Powell, 430 miles in six weeks. Back in the 1980s, she had gone horseback from the Mexican border to Canada, a six-month journey on the second day of which she was thrown from her mount, suffering a broken arm on impact. For most people, that mishap would have derailed the trip, or at least postponed it. Teresa was not most people. As fortune would have it, she found her way to a nearby ranch owned by a semiprofessional rodeo cowboy who happened to have some casting material handy; he typically used it on the calves he practiced roping, whenever the rope broke one of their legs. Calf-roping tended to result in a lot of broken legs, which healed relatively quickly when properly set. His expertise made for an impeccable cast on her arm, and he sent her on her way with some extra plaster, in case she needed to repeat the job herself.

But that was long ago, in what sometimes seemed to her another life entirely. During one of her last seasons as a lookout she had been poisoned by too much time spent in a tower infected with hidden mold. A subsequent tick bite bequeathed her a blood-borne pathogen and set her on an excruciating medical odyssey that lasted several years and only really ended after she spent long sessions in a hyperbaric chamber. At age 63, having lived hand-to-mouth for decades to feed her jones for adventure and avoid what she viewed as the suffocating expectations of the culture, namely marriage and motherhood, she had surprised herself by having a change of heart about marriage. In her capacity for solitude and all-around hardihood she made the perfect partner for John, but they had been granted only eleven months together. Now she was walking around with his ashes in a plastic bag and looking a little lost.

It felt like the right sort of day for spreading some of those ashes. The breeze was barely a whisper in the tops of the pines below us; their needle clusters glinted like pom-poms in the slanted sunlight. As the ribbons of ground fog began to lift and dissolve, we could see mountains way beyond the forest boundary, over in Arizona and down on the Mexican border. We both understood the gravity of what we were about to do and so we held off a while longer, not wanting to rush toward a reckoning. Instead we stood on the catwalk and watched the forest come to life, sometimes speaking quietly, sometimes pointing to something on the landscape, sometimes silently attentive as the hummingbirds buzzed around the feeder and the shadows shortened and the air began to warm. After a while I left Teresa alone with the view and went inside the tower to make myself some oatmeal with nuts and dried fruit, and a cup of coffee, extra-strong, with a generous pour of cream.

As I did so, the other lookouts began to call in service over the radio—first Jean on Black Mountain, then Hedge at Lookout Mountain, and on around the horn, one by one, Eagle Peak, Mogollon Baldy, Mangas Mountain, Fox Mountain, Saddle Mountain, Bearwallow, Hillsboro Peak—until all of us had been accounted for but me. Some days I liked to go first and others I preferred to go last, and often the ritual round of morning voices called to mind the first few lines of Gary Snyder's poem "The Lookouts":

Perched on their bare and windy peaks
They twitter like birds across the fractured hills
Equipped by science with the keenest tool—
A complex two-way radio, full of tubes.

The most alone, and highest in the land,
We trust their scrupulous vision to a man:

Or woman, I always added, adjusting the cadence to make the poem more inclusive, not to mention more accurate. The lookouts I admired most were women, so this zeal for accuracy was more than academic. Four of them—Teresa, Jean, Sara, and Rázik—counted a hundred fire seasons worth of experience altogether, a deep reservoir of knowledge about the country that, one had to believe, would never again be duplicated. Jean worked the loneliest of all the towers, seeing fewer visitors than any of the rest of us by far, sometimes only six or eight in a summer. Sara and Ráz split time equally at Baldy, since the hike in was so long—twelve miles—it didn't make sense for one of them to work the relief schedule of four days on and ten days off and spend half the time coming and going. Sara had spent more summers on her mountain—thirty-three straight—than John and I combined on ours; Ráz liked to joke that Sara knew the country so well she could tell you precisely which tree had started the fire. At twenty-four seasons of service herself, Ráz was no slouch when it came to understanding the lay of the land. She was 72 years old and as spry as most people half her age. I doubted I would be alive at 72, much less fit enough to hike twelve miles each way to work.

I joined the 9 AM chorus by pressing the transmit button on my Bendix-King VHF radio full of tubes and carefully enunciating, "Silver City dispatch, Signal Peak, in service." It felt peculiar to say words John had uttered on more than a thousand mornings. The name Signal Peak didn't feel right in my mouth, but that's where I was, so that's who I was, for the moment.

My spasm of discomfort passed as I moved into the daily routine of measuring the morning weather, a set of gestures identical for each of the ten lookouts on the forest: note the location and intensity of lightning in the previous twenty-four hours, eyeball the sky for its percentage of cloud cover, check the rain gauge for any precip since 9 the day before. Hold an anemometer into the wind, noting direction and range of speeds and maximum gust. Dip a sling psychrometer in distilled water, dampening the cotton sleeve that hugged its wet bulb; twirl the psychrometer's twin thermometers in the shade of the catwalk, producing readings from both the dry bulb (conventional air temperature) and wet bulb (cooler temperature created by evaporation from the dampened cotton). Discern the relative humidity from the difference between the two with the help of a handy chart. Write all this in the logbook in preparation for calling it in to the dispatcher.

"Silver City dispatch, Signal Peak, morning report," I announced, those two little words in the middle again sounding off—not just to me but to everyone listening.

O NCE I FINISHED ON THE RADIO, Teresa suggested a morning stroll. We descended the tower and walked down the trail until we came to an opening in the trees, on a ridge overlooking the rounded peaks of the Twin Sisters to the south. John had come there often with his wife, Miquette, back when they first staffed the tower, back when Miquette was still alive. In 1999, she had been hired as the primary lookout, he as her relief, and they both liked the view from a natural stone bench just below the top of the ridge: thick ponderosa pine rolling down the slopes of the Pinos Altos Range, giving way eventually to piñon-juniper country, and beyond it the cougar-colored grasslands. John spread some of Miquette's ashes in the clearing after her death, back in 2003.

Now it was his turn to join her.

In their last months together, John played caretaker while Miquette succumbed to cancer. This happened not long after my first summer as a lookout ended, so I didn't know him at the time, other than as one of many voices on my two-way radio. He later said it was the most difficult thing he had ever done, and in some ways the most meaningful.

Having been informed the disease was incurable, they embarked on a journey John called "hospice in a motor home." Thanks in part to an unexpected bequest from Miquette's godmother, the two of them had lived on the road for years, dropping anchor in different campgrounds for a week or a month at a time, moving across the mountains and deserts from New Mexico to Idaho; they didn't want their journey to end in some godforsaken institutional room. Ignoring the doctors' appalled warnings to the contrary, they packed up her crutches and oxygen tanks, her gauze patches and pill bottles, and set off toward a secret valley in California where they had stayed many times before. "It was as romantic, in its own intimate way, as a honeymoon," John later wrote of that week, in an essay he shared with friends.

They continued west to a campground on the Pacific coast, where the host, apprised of their situation, waived the two-week stay limit. As was their way, they continued to make connections until the very end. Folks stopped by to see whether they needed help, fellow RVers brought tapioca pudding to share with Miquette—part death watch, part social hour. When the end drew near they bowed to necessity and joined her family in Santa Cruz. "On New Year's Eve, with a sigh, Miquette slipped gently away," John wrote. "Outside the bedroom window, fireworks sparkled in the midnight sky."

Feeling an urge to bend his grief to some good purpose, John signed up to become an air angel, flying sick patients in need of emergency medical care to distant hospitals free of charge in his own private plane. He constantly reminded himself that, although the end had come too soon for her—she had died at 56—Miquette had lived out her dreams. As a little girl she loved horses so much she wanted to be one; she also fantasized about living in a tree house. After she met John they lived in the shadow of 14,000-foot peaks in Colorado, tucked amid a grove of aspens on the edge of a meadow, where they cared for a large herd of horses. Later they took up seasonal residence on Signal Peak, in a sort of deluxe tree house above the Gila. The timing and manner of her death had not undone the fact that hers had been, in many ways, a charmed life.

So had John's, mostly. As with all of us, there were areas of his personal history shadowed in varying degrees of darkness, but on the day of his death, age 62, he was happier than he had been in some time, excited to be planning a new honeymoon on which he would fly his Cessna Cardinal around the American West with Teresa, golfing at a different course in a different state each day—a major concession on her part, golf being far afield from her own interests, but what the hell, the things we do for love. Instead the plane was orphaned in a hangar at the Grant County Airport, and there would be no teeing off in Arizona one day and Utah the next, not to mention no more air-angel flights with him at the helm.

ON THE STONE BENCH, Teresa and I shared a few tears, a few laughs. John's laughter still echoed in our memories, and sometimes we merely felt like displaced conduits for it. Never parsimonious with his emotions, he would have appreciated the sight of us crying one minute and giggling the next—and sometimes both at once—as we sifted through what we remembered most vividly about him.

I sometimes thought of him as the blue-eyed gringo incarnation of a Mudhead Kachina, the drumming, dancing clown in Hopi ceremonies: partial to mischief and merriment, and the most gregarious lover of solitude I had ever known. His laughter, his most winning characteristic, tumbled forth in staccato waves, his belly shaking, his torso rocking back and forth from the hinge of his waist like a seesaw. He had a kind of bebop laugh that reminded me of Dizzy Gillespie's solo on "Salt Peanuts"—supple and exuberant, the individual notes crowding one another as if in a hurry to be free. When children visited his lookout tower, he delighted in showing them how he could make a flower of his lips by painting them with lipstick, drawing in hummingbirds for a drink of sugar water straight out of his mouth. I found the tube of cherry-colored Wet 'n Wild in the drawer where he kept his weather instruments; its gauche branding first made me laugh and then ruined me for half an hour with all it evoked of him.

The sight of that lipstick was nothing compared with my initial glimpse of his handwriting in the logbook, which detailed the major events of his last hours:

Noonish	Past lookout Bart Mortenson family arrives. Bart was a lookout here in the 70s. He honeymooned here
12:32	Smoke report: Azimuth 247° 30', Township 16S, Range 14W, Section 32—small white column—BART FIRE
12:39	Smoke more dense, still white color
12:57	Engine 672 on scene
13:00	Mortenson family spreads Bart's ashes north of tower. Nice singing of hymns drifting inside
13:05	BART FIRE getting a broader base. Lat/Long 33° 55' 32.1" × 108° 12' 46.8"
19:00	Out of service

Shortly after writing the words "Out of service" on the evening of June 7, 2014, he saddled his horse, Sundance, and set off on a ride along the Continental Divide Trail, passing by the spot where he had spread Miquette's ashes eleven years earlier. When he didn't call in service the next morning, two friends—his relief lookout, Mark Johnson, and his supervisor, Keith Mathes—set out ahead of a search-and-rescue team to hunt for him. The hunt did not last long. Both John and the horse were found where they fell; Sundance's massive bulk had crushed the torso of his rider. Neither betrayed signs of having struggled. Those of us who loved John kept telling ourselves that whatever the reason for the fall—a horse heart attack, the evidence suggested, although we would never know for sure—he had gone quickly, doing something he enjoyed, in a place he loved.

At least he died with his boots on, I told Teresa, inanely, when we met in the hours after his body was found.

"Not quite," she said. "Classic John: the bastard was wearing his tennis shoes. If he'd had his cowboy boots on, who knows, he might've been able to get out of the stirrups in time."

THOSE OF US WITH LONG EXPERIENCE sitting watch over the Gila sometimes joked that we were not so much fire lookouts anymore as morbid priests or pyromaniacal monks—officiants at an ongoing funeral for the forests as we had found them when we first assumed our posts. All of us had come seeking solitude, adventure, the romance of wild mountains, and a taste of the sublime; we got everything we had hoped for and more, including pyrotechnics on a landscape scale. The job never lasted long enough—six months maximum, more like four or five in a typical season—but it beat working down in the neon plastic valleys.

Nationwide, our numbers dwindled by the year, our sort of work a casualty of "development" and the schemes of the techno-titillated, who looked forward to the day when the last of us would be put out to pasture by satellites, drones, and high-definition infrared cameras linked with pattern-recognition software. We had been reduced from several thousand to a few hundred in the span of half a century, and the trend showed no sign of reversing; quite the contrary. The only question was how long we would last. Squinting in just the right light, after just the right number of drinks, I found it possible to envision an alternate reality in which I toiled alongside the rest of the creative class in the panopticon of the social-media surveillance economy, another insufferable white guy curating my personal brand—a tiny celebrity on a miniature stage—and art-directing amateur photo shoots of what I ate for lunch. That might still be my future. But not just yet. Not quite.

In the sunset days of a doomed vocation, I had lucked into a lineage of mountain mystics and lone rangers. We were paid in US dollars to read the meaning in clouds and discern the difference between positive and negative lightning. It seemed almost an oversight on the culture's part that the job still existed at all. Those of us who kept with it across the decades became walking repositories of bird-migration and weather patterns, fire history and trail conditions. For days and sometimes weeks on end we studied maps, performed seasonal maintenance on our facilities, and luxuriated in silence and solitude; some of us even learned to kiss hummingbirds. Then a storm moved over and the fires busted out, one or two or a dozen in an afternoon, and we earned our keep triangulating smokes, alerting crews to sudden changes in wind and fire behavior, guiding smokejumpers toward good trails on which to hike out after demob. It was hard to imagine jumpers on loan from Alaska or Montana, dropped from the sky into a remote place they had never seen before, getting that sort of intelligence from a high-def camera—*angle toward the ridge northwest of you above the scree field for about two-thirds of a mile, then look for the rock cairn at the base of a big Doug fir, and follow the trail east from there until it drops down to the creek bottom*—but the gadget fetishists never bothered to imagine that we offered more than merely a pair of eyes, that the evolving palimpsest of knowledge we accrued about the country might have some real and practical value beyond that of an adorable curio from an age before the world went virtual.

Those of us who worked on the Gila had the good fortune to watch over the forest that, for the sake of the health of the land, was allowed to burn more aggressively than any other in the Lower 48. We had witnessed the triumphs of progressive fire management, even played a small role in them, participants in a new pyromancy that no longer saw wildfire as a despised disruption of the natural order, a menace, a scourge. After most of a century of total suppression, the fire managers of the Gila National Forest had sculpted that new attitude into a strategy—let a few fires burn, when and where conditions were favorable, generally in the middle elevations of the wilderness areas, away from the settled edges of the forest—that helped preserve one of the healthiest ponderosa-pine stands in the Southwest.

The country outside the forest boundary was essentially a sacrifice zone to cattle grazing, denuded so thoroughly it was a study in desertification. The forest's fringes had been transformed as well, also badly overgrazed for more than a century, crisscrossed by roads and off-road-vehicle trails, and overgrown with unburned brush. In certain areas, woodcutting—for cooking, heating homes, making lumber, and smelting copper ore—had altered the forest structure, and throughout the region top predators, notably Mexican gray wolves and grizzly bears, had been the object of a relentless effort at zoöcide. Against all odds the wolves were making a comeback, but the grizzlies were likely gone forever.

The heart of the country nonetheless remained a land without roads, one of the wildest we had left, licked frequently by flame since at least the end of the Pleistocene and all the more beautiful and resilient for it. At McKenna Park, the place in the state of New Mexico farthest from pavement, you'd have to be lobotomized or a filthy aesthete not to sense something magical about the country: the scent of earth unbroken by human tools, a pine-oak savannah that called up a primeval feeling in the blood. The whole interwoven pattern of life there flourished amid frequent low-intensity burns; it had been and remained a fire-adapted ecosystem. The ponderosas dropped their lowest limbs to prevent fire climbing into their crowns, giving the forest a distinctive, open look. Nearly every living tree was blackened at its base—evidence of wildfire as handmaiden to evolution.

For close to four decades, the mantra on the Gila had been that fire was good, fire was necessary—the land had burned for millennia, after all, with no paramilitary force to stamp out smokes until the first years of the 20th century—but the size and character of the burns were changing. All across the planet, forests were undergoing an alarming die-off due to drought, disease, and beetle infestation, not to mention logging and slash-and-burn agriculture on an industrial scale—an apocalyptic acceleration of tree murder. Even in the world's first Wilderness, theoretically protected from destructive human activity, the effects of global warming were evident in the form of unstoppable megafires. They reinforced the fact that no place on earth was safely sealed off from the effects of human activity.

"One of the penalties of an ecological education is to live alone in a world of wounds," Aldo Leopold wrote seven decades ago. An ecological education is easier to come by in the 21st century than in Leopold's time; the penalty now is not to live alone with the burden of the knowledge—there is plenty enough company—but to feel helpless to stanch the losses foreordained by our pollution of the atmosphere with heat-trapping gases: losses of forests and ice, losses of habitat and species. We are in the midst of an irreversible ecocide. To fully grasp what our appetites have done to the nonhuman life of this planet would be to combust in guilt and grief.

In the two fire seasons preceding the summer of John's death, the forest saw the two biggest burns in its known history. First came the Whitewater-Baldy Fire in May 2012, which set a state record when two fires merged and burned five hundred square miles of the Mogollon Range, forcing Ráz and Sara off their mountain for most of the summer. It was followed eleven months later by the Silver Fire, a burn that chased me from my peak in a helicopter as half of the Black Range succumbed to flames. Taken together, the two fires roamed across nearly half a million acres. There wasn't much to do about them but marvel at the heat and smoke and what they wrought, which included, at their hottest, the incineration of the normally moist, dense woods of the high country: Douglas and corkbark fir, blue and Engelmann spruce.

The drier, warmer land below, on the flanks of the mountains and along the high mesas, was meant to burn frequently and had—the historical record suggested a couple times a decade was about average. But the big fires had taken the kind of old, big trees—living near 10,000 feet and above, and along the cool north-facing slopes slightly lower—that, according to tree-ring analysis, typically saw consuming fire just once every century or three, and then only in small patches. Now they were going away in massive stand-replacement events, and it felt silly to hope for their eventual return in a warming world. They were gone, and they weren't coming back.

On John's last day as a lookout, the open-ended memorial enlarged to include not just big old trees but one of our predecessors. It unnerved me to learn that John had saddled his horse and ridden to his death within hours of witnessing, out his tower window, those rituals honoring the memory of Bart Mortenson. The resonance of all the little details made for a paradoxical feeling, a retroactive sense of foreboding: the loved ones of a fellow lookout bearing the man's ashes to the mountain; the mention of that now poignant word, *honeymoon*; John's honoring the memory of the man by bestowing his name on a fire—*BART FIRE*—a mere seven hours before the fire in his own eyes went out.

THE FIRST THING YOU NOTICED about John were those lively, almost effervescent blue eyes. As lustrous as polished turquoise, they gave him an expression that appeared never to say no to the world, although that hadn't always been the case. "It took me some time to animate my face," he had once written, in a notebook discovered by Teresa after his death.

I thought I knew what he meant. When I learned he was a fellow Minnesotan, I tried once and only once to engage him on the subject, but he pivoted away so abruptly, with a look of such dread in those normally avid eyes, that I felt I had poked my finger in a wound. Only later would I learn that he had been present when his best friend accidentally killed himself while fooling around with a gun in the woods during the winter of their senior year of high school. The mere mention of the state where this had occurred was enough to make him recall the scene as if it had happened yesterday, although forty years had passed. He remembered just as vividly his parents' reaction to the tragedy, his father picking him up at the police station afterward, not saying a word as they drove home in terrible silence, and his mother turning away in disgust when he walked through the door, as if he had committed a murder.

It was not the sort of story one dropped as an icebreaker at parties. He trusted me with it, I suspect, because I first shared with him the fact that my brother had ended his life with a bullet from a semi-automatic assault rifle. Sometimes you just have a feeling about people, and from the beginning of our acquaintance I judged him to be the kind of man who was capable of absorbing such knowledge with sensitivity and grace. From the very beginning, in fact: I shared my brother's story with him the first time I saw him face-to-face, at an end-of-season gathering of lookouts in summer 2003.

Come to think of it, I suppose you could say I dropped it as an icebreaker at a party. Mark Hedge, the resident sage on Lookout Mountain, had invited four of us to his place at Elephant Butte for beer around the backyard fire pit; for some in attendance, including me and John, it would be our first chance to connect faces with familiar voices on the radio. That was the day John spread Miquette's ashes near the tower where they had lived four summers together. He knew he was going to spend time with other lookouts that evening, and although he hadn't met us all in person yet, the thought of our company gave him the courage to do a thing he had been putting off for months. Within an hour of having shaken hands, we were both in tears over the loss of people we had loved. We began in mutual candor; it would have felt phony to proceed any other way thereafter.

Shared some months later, his story of having paid witness to a friend's death by gunshot revealed that we were blood brothers of a sort. Each of us, in the wake of a bullet's destruction, had checked into the guilt suite at the Hotel Sorrow and re-upped for a few hundred weeks, he at 17, I at 23.

"I reviewed my life and it was also a river," Herman Hesse wrote, in the voice of Siddhartha, a sentence that stayed with me through the years. Whenever I recalled it I felt an impulse to revise it for my own purposes and replace the word *river* with the word *fire*: *I reviewed my life and it was also a fire.* My life was more like a series of fires, each of which moved through similar phases, from a thunderous moment of ignition—the lightning strike of a brother's suicide, the incendiary dissolution of a marriage—to the full flaring heat of grief, followed by a long, slow cooling, a landscape of ashen remains, and, finally, purgation and rebirth. It occurred to me more than once to share my plagiarized sentiment with John, including him in it—*I reviewed our lives and they were also fires*—but I never had, and now I never would. I had erred in assuming that tomorrow remained a perpetual possibility for that combination of elements forged in friendship and known as *us*. For me, tomorrow might still come. Probably would, in fact. For him, and for us, there would be no such thing.

S HORTLY AFTER THE FATAL GUNSHOT, John left the exurbs of Minneapolis and began a life of travel and adventure that took him across the country and around the world, including a yearlong trip through Mexico and South America and a stint of expatriate living in Spain. His work life included an exotic mélange of duties: bartender, gentleman rancher, private investigator, PR man for a race-car team, claims adjuster for Lloyd's of London. At the time of his death, he was president and part owner of an airplane-repair shop. The job about which he liked to reminisce most involved his misadventures as a deputy marshal in Telluride, Colorado, where he and his boss, committed to gentler forms of justice than the code books called for, adopted the motto *Better us than the real guys.*

He possessed a colorful and mysterious backstory and lots of fancy toys even as he cultivated a reputation as a midwestern penny-pincher, partial to torn blue jeans and thrift-store sweatshirts, liable to haggle over the cost of just about anything. He surrounded himself with all the trappings of old-school machismo, the whole suite of midlife-crisis totems—airplane, Jeep, motorcycle, Pantera sportscar, GT40 race car—while conducting his emotional life in the most open and vulnerable way possible. He liked to fly high and drive fast; he liked sitting in one place for months, watching mountains. He lived simply in a house of four hundred square feet; he owned a forty-foot mobile home he liked to call his "land yacht."

The last time I saw him alive it was with our mutual pal Mark Johnson, John's relief lookout on Signal Peak. My girlfriend and I joined John and Mark for dinner and a beer, and when we were through Mark was the first to leave. Before he did so, John opened his arms as if welcoming a good-bye hug; Mark leaned in, and John gave him a kiss full on the lips. All this, appropriately enough, at a bar called Wrangler's, which catered to the clientele one would expect from a place by that name. It struck me as the first time in my entire life I had witnessed two straight dudes kiss each other on the lips with real affection and no self-consciousness in a public place. The surprise of bearing witness to it was surpassed only by the surprise of realizing I was a little bit jealous.

On the other hand, when I mentioned John's death to the first friend I encountered after hearing the news, my friend said: "You know, that guy was a real asshole." Stuart said that John had come into his metal-fabrication shop one day, seeking a quote on a minor welding project. When Stuart gave him one, John blanched and began—cheapskate that he was—to bargain for a lower price. Stuart countered that he had given him a fair price: take it or leave it. John grumbled in a way that left Stuart feeling abused and insulted. John left and never returned.

More even than haggling for better deals, the man loved needling bureaucratic authority. Even as a lowly agency employee (pay grade GS-4) with no health insurance, no retirement benefits, and a merely seasonal appointment (forestry technician—lookout), he wrote long, deeply researched letters of complaint to the chief of the US Forest Service about the waste of running reconnaissance flights over a forest already covered by the eyes of ten lookouts. "Dear Chief Tidwell," one such missive began, "I am a fellow Forest Service employee. I work as a fire lookout . . . rest assured my office is nicer than yours." After this cheeky opening, he spent nine pages and several thousand words attacking the agency's rationale for using expensive, accident-prone aircraft to detect fires and guide slurry planes in a place such as the Gila. His objections encompassed both the practical—wasteful spending of tax dollars, leaded-gas emissions over the wilderness—and the philosophical, the latter grounded in the knowledge that the landscape we loved and claimed as part owners along with the rest of the American public was stolen from the Apache in a genocidal war. With the red man subdued and removed, red flames had been cast as a savage force that could be tamed only by efforts on a military model. Seen in that light, firefighting—with helicopters, slurry bombers, and paratrooper smokejumpers—was simply a way of perpetuating the endless war on the land. Despite a reputation as the most forward-thinking forest in the country when it came to fire, the Gila still suppressed more than 90 percent of new wildfire starts. Some old habits die hard, none more so than those involving the tools of warfare, funded by unlimited sums of emergency money.

A part of John hoped, vainly as it turned out, that he would be called on to answer for his litany of heresies by the "chain of command." Meanwhile he remained on a friendly, first-name basis with the aviation officers of the Gila, who always said hello via the air-to-ground frequency when they flew over his mountain on their redundant recon missions. He thought their work bogus and profligate, not to mention needlessly risky with human life, but that didn't prevent him from liking the people who did it, or they him. He loved to fly circles over beautiful country—and had to admit it was quite the caper for the flyboys and flygirls to have found a way to get paid for doing precisely that.

ABOUT TEN DAYS into my hitch as his stand-in, I hiked down to the scene of his death to pay homage. For reasons I couldn't fully explain, probably having to do with both my fear of death and the allure of it—the big dark, the long sleep—I wanted to spend some time in the place where he had breathed his last breath.

Over the years, I had become, quite in contrast to anything I had ever dreamed—who would imagine such a thing ahead of time?—a connoisseur of burn scars. My first such forays involved backpack trips to the interior of the Gila's wilderness areas, but more recently the burns appeared inclined to come to me.

The earth where John fell to his death had burned in the Signal Fire a little more than a month earlier. His last big wildfire as a lookout, it had left another new burn scar calling out for exploration. The smoke started on Mother's Day afternoon, when target shooters threw their spent shells in a hollow stump just off the Signal Peak Road. The heat from the cluster of shells set the stump to smoldering, and it smoldered long enough to ignite the grass and pine needles surrounding it. (The shooters slipped away and were never identified.) Aided by steady winds at thirty miles per hour and up, the grass fire quickly swept into the timber; once in the treetops it became a running crown fire, with flame lengths of fifty feet and more. These sorts of fires—started accidentally by humans—were often the hottest kind, because they tended to happen not, as with lightning, in conjunction with rain, but rather on dry, windy days, early in the season, before the summer monsoon greened the grass and brought the fuel moistures back up. On windless days the goofuses who were careless with fire tended to catch their own mistakes before the fires spread. On windy days they turned tail and ran, leaving the fight to the Forest Service.

The Signal Fire ran up the flank of the mountain in a hurry, wind-driven all the way. Only the arrival of a backdoor cold front that first night stopped it from growing ten times larger than its final tally of 5,484 acres. Overnight, the humidity rose and temperatures dropped into the twenties; more crucially, the prevailing west wind changed to a light east one, turning the fire back on itself—but not before John and Teresa were forced to flee down the mountain on foot. After their departure, the fire crested the ridge at the base of the tower, and the heat half-melted the flamingos John had arranged in wry imitation of a suburban lawn. The fire essentially died there, leaving one side of the mountain green, the other black, with malformed pink plastic birds marking the boundary.

Two weeks later, the fire was cold when three students from a local charter school flew over the burn scar in a private plane, assessing the changes to a forest transect they had laid out for a class project in eco-monitoring. It was the last thing they would do with their promising young lives. "On May 23, 2014, at 1553 mountain daylight time, a Raytheon G36 airplane, N536G, impacted terrain near Silver City, New Mexico," the National Transportation Safety Board report stated. "The private pilot and three passengers were fatally injured. The airplane was destroyed."

The airplane was returning from a local flight and the pilot flew a tight down-wind leg for landing on runway 35, possibly due to a direct crosswind in excess of 20 knots. During the base turn, the airplane overshot the final course, and the pilot used at least 60 degrees of bank to correct the airplane back on course and over the runway. The airplane then bounced and touched down at least 20 knots above the manufacturer's published approach speed with about 1,810 ft remaining on the runway. The airplane's airspeed began to rapidly decrease, but then several seconds later, the airplane's airspeed increased as the pilot rejected the landing. The airplane did not gain significant altitude or airspeed then began a slight right turn. The airplane's roll rate then sharply increased, and the airplane quickly descended, consistent with a stall, before colliding with a transmission wire and terrain. Examination of the airframe and engine did not reveal any pre-impact anomalies that would have precluded normal operation. Strong, variable, gusty wind, with an environment conducive to the formation of dry microbursts, was present at the airport at the time of the accident. Several lightning strikes were recorded in the vicinity of the accident site around the time of the accident. It is unknown if the presence of lightning or wind impacted the pilot's inflight decision-making in the pattern, on approach, or during the attempted go-around. The circumstances of the accident are consistent with an in-flight encounter with a strong tailwind and/or windshear during climbout after the rejected landing.

John had reported the presence of the small fixed-wing near his tower that afternoon, in keeping with lookout protocol; he later reported the smoke plume from the crash, aware from the moment he saw it what it meant. The deaths of those kids, coming so soon after they had circled his tower, shook him badly. Two were 16 years old, the other 14. All were members of the Aldo Leopold High School science team, which had won the Envirothon state championship six weeks earlier. A thousand people turned out for their memorial.

The young man among them, Michael Mahl, had been a gifted guitarist who also played drums, ukulele, and mandolin; he performed most Sundays at a church in Silver City led by his pastor grandfather. The two young women, Ella Jaz Kirk and Ella Myers, had participated in a writing workshop I conducted at the school not long before their death. Ella Myers wrote a novel at the age of 12 and had been accepted at an elite film school in Chicago; Ella Kirk, the youngest, played violin and piano, wrote her own songs, and collected more than 6,400 signatures on her self-authored petition to protect the Gila River from a billion-dollar dam project cooked up by scheming bureaucrats in Santa Fe. She testified about the issue before a state legislative committee with a poise I doubt I could have matched. Those kids' lives, seemingly limitless in their potential, were, in a way, casualties of the fire as surely as the mixed conifer on the north slope of the mountain. That John died inside the burn scar shortly after the crash only compounded the fire's eerie aftereffects: loss layered on loss.

From the mountain one could see almost the entire burn, the pattern it had chewed across the land quite obvious: west to east, with an uphill push to the top of the divide along the southern perimeter. It was far from the most spectacular fire I had witnessed, but it had more personal resonance than most. It was to be the last smoke on which I collaborated with John; I gave him an azimuth on it from my vantage, so he could pinpoint how far north of his tower it was before he bailed off the mountain. Now, staring at the burn scar day after day up close, I felt as if I would be shirking a duty if I didn't venture into it. One evening, after signing off the radio, I decided it was time for a walk through the ash.

It didn't take long to discover the scene of John's death; the smell tipped me off from fifty yards away. The body of Sundance still lay where it fell, and his bay-colored hide stood out in a landscape that was now monochrome, the bare earth and fire-scarred trees streaked and daubed with white vulture droppings, like a halfway-finished Pollock painting. John's body had been retrieved by Forest Service friends and colleagues, but rules and regs did not call for the removal of a half-ton of horseflesh from national forestland, and the birds had made a feast of it. In the afternoons, I sometimes watched them circling the ridge southeast of the tower, as many as two dozen at a time riding thermals over the crest of the divide, spinning in languid gyres, dark against the light-blue sky—lazy-looking but never not vigilant. Sort of like lookouts.

The trail ran along a steep slope on the southern edge of the burn. Sundance had fallen hard to the downhill side, his neck bent around a charred tree trunk. In the two weeks since, his carcass had shrunk until the hide draped over the bones like a tattered blanket. Beneath that blanket, inside the rib cage, something scratched and scrabbled—something alive. I stood and listened for a while, touched in some very old way, even sort of honored to eavesdrop on the process of flesh reentering the food chain by the traditional method. The sound said all you needed to know about the pickins being slim: a dry scraping, signifying that the carcass had been worked over pretty well already. I tossed a small rock at it, then another, half-fearing the appearance of a tiny bear cub, which would imply the presence of its mother nearby.

Instead a vulture poked its head from inside the horse's body cavity. It crawled out into the light, glanced over its shoulder at me, beat its heavy wings, and took flight through the bare branches of the ghost forest: meal interrupted.

The turkey vulture, a study in paradox: from a distance so graceful, gliding on invisible currents, air riffling its fingerlike wing tips; at close range so hideous, with its raw red head, greasy brown feathers, and contemptuous yellow eyes. Misfortune its sustenance, death what's for dinner. "Your ass is somebody's else's meal," Gary Snyder wrote, in his essay "The Etiquette of Freedom," and more than once I had imagined my corpse—after an accidental fall from my fire tower—picked clean by *Cathartes aura*, ensuring my remains would soar one last time over mountains before falling back to earth as scavenger's excrement. What can I say? The days are long in a lookout tower. But not until that moment, as I stood over the bag of bones called Sundance, had I known by name a creature who'd passed through a vulture's digestive system.

It occurred to me to wonder whether John might have chosen the same fate, had he been given the option. It would have been like him to skip the expense of cremation.

A PECULIAR THING HAPPENS once you've been a lookout for many seasons. Radio protocol demands that you forgo your given name and identify yourself by the name of your peak. For several months each year you are not Sara Irving or Rázik MaJean, Teresa Beall or Mark Hedge, Jean Stelzer or John Kavchar; you are the name of a mountain. Mogollon Baldy. Bearwallow. Lookout Mountain. Black Mountain. Signal Peak. The longer you keep the job, the more intimately your identity becomes entwined with that mountain.

At the same time, in our shared vigilance, scattered across the sky-island ridge tops, we come to feel ourselves a part of more than just a mountain, a part of something grand and dignified, a club of splendid misfits, delightfully at odds with the drift of the culture. Eventually the voices of our fellow freaks on peaks become aural talismans, sources of comfort and connection amid a sometimes enigmatic solitude.

It's not merely the radio that provokes this transformation. By living and working where we do we become intimate with the moods of a wild and moody place, its flora and fauna, its susceptibility to extreme weather; we discover which of the north-face snowbanks melts last, where water collects in the rainy season, which trees lure convergent lady beetles by the thousands until their bark turns a writhing orange. We learn the songs of birds and the names of flowers, the spooky thrill of monsoon-season mornings waking up inside the clouds. We discover where to find food in the time of ripeness—wild raspberries, prickly gooseberries—and where other creatures find theirs.

Our terse radio commo ratifies an evolving external reality. The work has made of the mountains a gift to us, and we honor this gift by assuming and intoning their names. John had been Signal Peak; Signal Peak had been John, for every summer of the new millennium, just as Mogollon Baldy had been Sara and Ráz, and Lookout Mountain Hedge, and Black Mountain Jean. No matter how many times I repeated those two little words, I couldn't make them comfortable in my own voice, calling in service each morning, calling in my smoke and weather reports. I was not Signal Peak and never would be. Only John could eyeball the sky and with whimsical precision call in a morning report of 17.5 percent cloud cover. Only John could get away with naming a harmless end-of-season smoke the Jell-O Fire. To have tried such a trick would have marked me as a pretender.

His presence permeated the two hundred square feet of penthouse real estate where I cooked and slept and kept watch that June, and sometimes I had to leave the tower and wander the mountain for twenty minutes just to get away from him. He was there in the vase of plastic flowers set on the windowsill; he was there in the bag of Smokey Bear lapel pins kept handy as swag for visitors with kids. Even something as simple as a can of refried beans in the pantry reminded me of our routine for Continental Divide Trail thru-hikers, those creatures of seemingly limitless fortitude whose route brought them first to my mountain, then his, on their journey from Mexico to Canada. By the time they reached me they had traveled 100 miles through the desert—the bare beginning of their 3,000-mile journey along the spine of the Rockies. If they arrived at my tower after quitting time, I would offer a swig of tequila as we looked upon the country they had traveled to get there and the route that lay ahead. Once they returned to the trail, whether that same evening or the next morning, I would radio John and let him know visitors were on their way, ETA twenty-four hours, give or take, and he would do the prep work on a batch of nachos. We had never met a thru-hiker who wasn't tickled by the gift economy of the Gila's high peaks: aperitif at my tower, appetizer at John's. All they had heard of the place were rumors of its rough beauty and its capacity for inflicting bodily punishment, and here they were, being treated like visiting dignitaries.

THE MOMENT HAD ARRIVED for John to become one with the mountain. Teresa opened the plastic bag. We dipped our hands in his ashes, extracted pinches between our fingertips, let them float off below us, toward a cluster of surviving century plants. His ashes mingled there with the ashes of the Signal Fire, his final form mingling with his final major burn; within weeks, perhaps even days, a good rain would flush some of the ash and loose soil down drainage, a nutrient recharge for the banks of the creek bottoms and, for a bit of his remains, one last ride through a piece of country he had known better than nearly anyone alive.

I was surprised to find myself reminded of the Catholic masses of my childhood, when the priest, arms uplifted, would intone over the Eucharist the words of the doomed savior at his last supper: *Take this, all of you, and eat, for this is my body. . . . Do this in memory of me.* John had been intimate with those same rituals, and we had talked about how one is never quite a former Catholic, only a recovering Catholic, the liturgy having been absorbed on an almost molecular level by our spongy young minds. For us, the metaphors had been more enduring than the faith, none more so than those of Ash Wednesday, when our foreheads had been traced by the priest's thumb, the cross-shaped smudge a reminder of mortality and mourning, a harbinger of what lay in store for us all:

For you are dust, and to dust you shall return . . .

Simultaneously—unprompted by word or gesture—Teresa and I each licked our fingers, wanting to take a bit of him into ourselves. I suppose some might view this as macabre, perhaps even some kind of health hazard, but we had both inhaled the smoke of huge burns, as had John during his fifteen years on the mountain. The taste of ash on the tongue was becoming more familiar all the time, as historic fires devoured the mixed conifer of the Southwestern high country. The forests would evolve and become something else—spruce and fir succeeded by aspen, pine replaced by locust and oak. What they had been for millennia was now, like John, a memento etched in flame.

As the day's heat increased, a few proto-cumulus began to form. Teresa and I tossed another pinch of John into the air, watched the motes drift and swirl downslope on the breeze. We shared a bitter laugh at the irony of her having finally found a man she cared to stand by for the long run—only to have him maroon her at the altar in the most theatrical fashion possible.

She gestured at the sky: "Looks like you're about to be in business." We hugged and said good-bye, and she set off down the trail, back toward home, where she would spend the next year and a half in a longer and more complicated relationship with John's possessions than she had with the man himself.

Her departure left me alone to the spectacle in the sky. And what a spectacle: the ancient drama of monsoon moisture streaming north off the Gulf of Mexico, meeting the furnace of the desert and rising over the mountains, the resulting cumulus clusters expanding like popcorn kernels, their bottoms slowly darkening and tendrils of virga beginning to fall, and finally the first hot flash of a ground strike in the middle distance. By midafternoon, dry lightning jabbed the mesas to the north every few seconds, and new smokes were popping up. I called in three in the span of an hour. Still unfamiliar with the terrain from John's vantage point, I misplaced one of them by two miles. The crew sent to suppress it found it anyway, in plenty of time.

That evening, off the clock and out of service, I took a couple of pulls from the tequila bottle John had left behind. I uncapped his tube of lipstick and made myself up in the reflection of his handheld signal mirror. Lips puckered, a sad clown waiting for a hummingbird's kiss, I couldn't help thinking that the man I would have liked to ask about the contours of the country, the man who could have alleviated my ignorance, was forever unavailable. No longer up above the country keeping watch, he was now a part of it—and a part of me. +

JENNIFER MURPHY, *WHITE GOD'S EYE*. 2010, STICKS AND YARN. COURTESY CLINT ROENISCH GALLERY.

LONGVIEWERS

Rebecca Schiff

MOMMY AND DADDY hate the other street. The other street used to be just another street, but now it wants to give us its traffic, to cause us pain. Now Mommy and Daddy host meetings in our house like it is union times. If it were union times, we wouldn't have a house, or artichoke appetizers for the other angry people, but the spirit would be the same. I've never seen Mommy and Daddy so worked up. Usually, they're at work. They just go to work and they hardly have friends. Not like me, who's always on the phone, dampening the little holes. They got me Line 2, and when it's for me, they yell, "Line 2!" like it's my name. I never even noticed the traffic on our street. I don't even drive.

"You still call them that?" says Kira, a friend who also has her own line. "I stopped calling my parents Mommy and Daddy when I learned to tie my shoes."

"You're so mature," I say. "Can you give me maturity lessons?"

Daddy tells me to get off the phone, it's time for Save-Our-Street strategy.

Daddy, he's incensed about the other street, his neck bullfrogging out over his tie. He's not even loosening the tie anymore, just gets home from work and starts dialing his new friends, Bruce and Bruce, the other save-the-street fanatics. Daddy's got a widower friend now, too, and the never-married Vietnamese woman with a Long Island accent who gardens. She plants bulbs, waves him over for the update.

"They've got a lawyer now," she hisses, smushing dirt. "That's OK," he says. "We've got the mafia."

Daddy jokes, but only with our street. With the other street, he makes a point of racing down it, pounding the horn. He goes to town meetings and curses the mayor, whose name is May Hamburger. May Hamburger is in somebody's pocket on the other street. They claim their street, Longview, is too narrow to have two-way traffic. Last spring, they say, a child almost died. Our street, Hillview, is wider; a thoroughfare, a boulevard. Hillview can accommodate.

But Mommy says they're just worried about property values. The Longviewers, she says, only care about money.

"That kid did need stitches," I say.

"Longviewers are selfish. They could care less if we live or if we die." She's folding chairs.

"How much did our house cost?" I ask.

"A lot," says Daddy.

"It's about safety," she says, plunking a chair against a chair. "It's about not getting stepped on. You know, the Longviewers hired a lawyer."

"This is like the Balkans," I say. "This is how ethnic conflict gets started."

We did ethnic conflict last year in Integrated Studies, which is English and Social Studies combined in a classroom with an accordion divider. This year, we're reading our thirty-seventh Steinbeck and getting quizzed on kamikaze pilots. Did they:

A) Drop an atomic bomb on Hiroshima?

B) Fly on wind power alone?

C) Undertake suicide missions on behalf of the Japanese government during World War II?

D) Strafe Longview?

At least we're not learning about Helen Keller anymore. Sometimes I write invisible letters on Kira's hand in Integrated Studies. T-H-I-S (flat palm) S-U-C-K-S. We're not making fun of Helen Keller, just using her techniques to get by. We have our own handicaps. Boys who crack Helen Keller jokes ignore our collective lack of breast. They're probably from Longview.

No, Kira doesn't live on the other street. She's just a friend from the town. Kira thinks my parents are "awesome." Once, I think, she saw them kissing.

AWESOME DADDY is now shouting "furthermore" into a tape recorder. "He's losing it," says Mommy, not at all scared.

Did he ever have it? I really don't know. In the photo albums, he looks peaceful, with a fatter tie. The albums are pre-me. Mommy and Daddy slide around under loose plastic flaps, in front of trolley cars, the Dead Sea. Maybe trolley cars are the answer to the problems of street. Maybe monorail. In Technology, we cut out articles about electric cars, then paste the articles onto paper a little bigger than the articles. Electric-car articles hang around the room, next to articles about maglev trains.

Kira and I sand a lot in Technology. Our bridges are almost soft. But hers, with tighter scaffolding and a two-pyramid base, holds more pebbles. My bridge is not strong. I keep working on it. It keeps breaking. I keep fixing it. The bridge project is a way to pass the quarter until it is time for the end of wood. Then we have Math. Math seems to be about fractions canceling each other out, about objects in space, and the cute fish of infinity.

"Furthermore," Daddy repeats, almost kissing the tape recorder. "Furthermore, if the town chooses to make Longview Road a one-way street without a fair hearing, then we, the residents of Hillview Road, will be forced to take matters into our own hands and, in the tradition of Martin Luther King and Gandhi, take unlawful actions against an unjust government." He clicks off.

"Are you crazy?" asks Mommy, now afraid. In between "He's losing it" and "Are you crazy?" lies a whole sea of meaning.

"I'm mailing it to Hamburger tomorrow," he says. "If she doesn't respond before Wednesday, we're taking the street."

"Our own street?"

Daddy looks around for a padded envelope, and sees instead a potential ally, the girl who just aced her test on India.

"Hey, punko," he says. "Want to show Longview what we're made of?"

I think of the post-me albums, the diapers, the boys who make diaper jokes about Gandhi.

"Do you want me to get hit by a car on purpose?"

"No, just clean up your room before the meeting tomorrow."

"They're not going to go in my room."

o   o   o

M Y BED'S BEEN MADE. I trot downstairs, sling around the banister at the base. I pile some hot artichoke on a saltine. The chairs are out, evenly staggered, Mommy style. She's very exacting about the chairs.

"Good job, Mom."

Mom? It just comes out, her new name. Is this how it happens? One day you're "Mommy, change me, feed me, sprinkle talc all over my naked body," the next day you're complimenting her on folding-chair spacing. Mommy doesn't notice.

"I need to review the talking points," she says. "Don't eat all the dip before people get here."

People get here. The gardener lady's wearing lipstick, maybe hoping to meet another enraged single. She's dreaming, though, because except for me and the widower, it's all furious couples in sweaters.

Daddy has maps, crudités, an easel.

"That was my easel," I say, to nobody. Nobody asked to borrow it, either.

"The morning commute won't be affected by the one-way choke-hold Longview is imposing, since cars can still use both Longview and Hillview to go west," he says, drawing parallel sedans going west. "But we want to get some folks out to protest Longview in the mornings, too. Bruce? Lillian?

"The evenings are when we have our real battle. As the streets parallel, we will get all of Longview's eastbound commuter traffic." He draws a fat line of trucks trying to go east.

"Not on our watch!" screams a Bruce.

"Not our kids," says a wife, pointing at me. There's applause. I represent something, a kid who might run into the street, basted by a car that should have been on Longview.

"She knows not to run into the street," says Daddy. "But, as I said in the tape I sent City Hall, some kids don't. And that's why we're not going to let these Longviewers commute in peace, day or night, until we get this one-way farce reversed and traffic is flowing freely on both streets in both directions again!" He draws cars going in both directions.

"Sign up for a morning or evening shift depending on your work schedule. Stay-at-home moms, we need you right now."

Mommy calls them nonworking mothers.

o   o   o

"I WISH MY PARENTS CARED ABOUT SOMETHING," says Kira. She's using ketchup packets to make a rag look bloody for a skit we have to do about *The Pearl.* She's going to play the mother and me the father. A doll is playing our baby. A Tic Tac is playing the pearl.

"You live on a cul-de-sac," I say. "What's the problem?"

"My dad has no interest in community service."

I don't mind playing the father. I've borrowed one of Daddy's old jackets, and I'm roughing it up with a stapler. I'm going to need a mustache. Luckily, I have no breasts. Kira's costume is from our linen closet. Her hair's in braids.

"The kids who got *Of Mice and Men* are really lucky," she says, trying to make our doll look deader. "I'd kill for that one."

BOTH PHONE LINES are busy over the weekend. One of the Bruces is getting divorced. He'll be departing our street for a condo, a support group.

"I'm losing a real soldier," says Daddy.

There was the time this Bruce stayed up half the night coming up with the perfect clipart for the "Hillview Is Not a Highway" flyer, the time he called Mayor May a cunt. After a while Daddy just says, "A soldier," and Mommy and I fill in the rest of his sad.

Over on Line 2, Kira sheds her uterine lining for the first time. My bridge almost collapses with the news. My uterine lining remains intact. Happily married Bruce calls on Line 1 to talk to Daddy, now his one remaining Bruce, suddenly the only Bruce he can count on.

The town, for some reason, is not moved by the tape.

"Do you know what this means?" Daddy laughs, maybe thrilled to be ignored. "Hamburger wants war. Are you ready to mobilize?"

We're sitting around the kitchen table Tuesday evening. Mommy's drowning a tea biscuit in decaf. I'm coloring in my *maison* for French. I draw *mon téléphone* in *ma chambre.*

"*La Ligne Deux,*" I write.

"I'll call Bruce," he says.

"I don't know," says Mommy.

"I have a Pakistan ditto," I say. "But then I can help."

Help means collating the new flyers, practicing our chants. The new flyers say ONE WAY? NO WAY!

"I have to be at work early tomorrow," says Mommy later. She's in her nightgown, under her lamp. He's pacing the den, pretending to yell at cars. "So keep an eye on him on Longview," she says. "Don't let him do anything crazy."

"If he tries to do something crazy, how will I stop him?"

"Just tell him to stop."

WEDNESDAY AM, Daddy and I are standing in the shoulder of the other street, minivan gusts whipping our ONE WAY? NO WAY! signs back into our chests. Daddy's scanning for his friends. Never-married gardener is a no-show. Happily married Bruce is not present.

The cars just go west. There's not much to see.

The widower friend shows up wearing his flannel jacket, dusted with dog hair. He and Daddy sort of grip each other hello, and then he leaves. We wait. A couple of women in terry cloth walk by, but we're not sure if they're Longviewers or Hillviewers or just power walkers.

"Maybe tomorrow I'll bring Kira, so we have more people."

"The whole street's in denial," says Daddy. "People completely disregarded the sign-up sheet. The stay-at-home moms stayed at home. But wait until they see how much traffic our street eats tonight. We'll stand in front of our house with signs. I'll make extra copies at work, so everyone has one to hold."

LE MATIN PROCHAIN, LE MÊME. Except Daddy makes me and Kira sing a song. It has to do with sticking to a union till the day we die. We sang it last night on the sidewalk in front of our house. Daddy passed out lyrics. Mommy and I didn't need them. The union song is from a cassette Daddy keeps in the car for long car trips. We have other tapes, but Daddy never plays them. What he does play now are cassettes from Line 1's answering machine—Sorry, Alan, work's been crazy, tae kwon do, Karen caught the flu. Mommy urges Daddy to delete, but he's starting a list by the phone.

"Not flu season yet!" it says.

FRIDAY MORNING, I lie in bed for a few minutes after I wake up, sliding the lump under my left nipple. It seems wider than usual, wider than the right. I scramble to my desk, flip through the index of *Exploring Life Science* until I find Puberty, female.

"Breast bud and papilla swell and a small mound is present; areola diameter is enlarged."

This is it, this is Puberty, female.

A T ASSEMBLY, Kira tells me she can't come anymore. Assembly's in the gym. It's Croatia Day. Puffed-sleeved maidens wave handkerchiefs while the teachers shush us. Every last Friday of the month, we're herded into the bleachers to disrespect dancers from politically unstable lands.

"It's only been two days," I say. "We haven't even done civil disobedience yet."

"Why do you keep touching your breast?"

"I'm not. Why can't you? Is your mom scared?"

"No. Your dad's—"

The dancers' clogs make a sudden racket on the shellacked floor.

"What? My dad's what?"

"Your dad's awesome. But I don't live in that neighborhood."

M ONDAY MORNING, we stand on a lawn on Longview instead. Even the widower's given up, gone back to his usual routine, transferring photographs of his late wife out of albums that have lost their stick. Our signs have wrinkled, curled. They're already mementos of this time.

"Longview is kind of scary without sidewalks, Daddy."

"They could build sidewalks," snaps Daddy. "There's certainly enough room on their lawns. Then they'd have sidewalks."

"Where's the lady who gardens?" I say.

"Who?" he says.

"Bruce never comes."

"He's redoing his dining room."

"What's wrong with his dining room?"

"Gene Flusser!"

The driver of a passing car is a famous Longviewer, the one in bed with May Hamburger. Daddy drops his sign and gives Flusser's bumper the finger.

"Is the finger in the tradition of Martin Luther King?" I ask.

"This one is," he says. He leaves the finger up, for everybody. I put mine up, aiming it at the other street and also a little at him.

I guess we're showing Longview what we're made of.

We're made of cells. We're made of fatty tissues, which we either fear or desire, depending on where they deposit. We get labeled in text-books—organ, organelle. We give traffic the finger.

Except traffic must have seen the finger, because Gene Flusser's walking back, from kind of far. He can't drive back because the street's one way.

"Daddy, stop," I say.

"Stop what?" he says, tucking his middle finger back into his fist.

"He's coming."

"I see him—Gene!"

"Alan! Aren't you cold standing here?" asks Flusser.

"We're staying warm," says Daddy.

"Who's this young lady?"

"She's a fighter."

It's all very friendly, Longview, Hillview. What the view is of, nobody can say.

"Shouldn't you be in school?" says Flusser, extending a handshake to me.

"I have a note." One of my hands rests on my jacket where the new breast should be. The other shoots out to shake. "But I'm learning a lot out here. You guys could use some sidewalks. Why'd you get out of the car, Mr. Flusser?"

"I forgot my lunch, so I'm going back to get it." He doesn't even look at our signs.

I'M ON YEARBOOK NOW. I write poems about assemblies, come up with captions for boys who ignore me.

Kira and I didn't stop being friends because of the street. We're still friends. Now we're crying about the Joads. Now we're sanding boats. They will float on half an inch of water in a stoppered sink. They will never know the sea.

Mommy has a new enemy: the phone company.

"Thieves," she says, highlighting my calls on the bill. But her heart's not in the hate. The folding chairs stay folded in the basement. My easel stays folded.

Daddy's not doing mornings on Longview anymore. He decided it was best to conserve our energy for our own street, because people in gridlock are more likely to be sympathetic. He's not doing evenings on our street anymore either, though, except that he sits in gridlock with the others on his way home from work.

But walking home, sometimes I think I see him, one block away, planted on our sidewalk, a man with salt and pepper ringing his bald spot, a man with a windbreaker, Longview's worst nightmare, the only man with enough love to turn the tide the other way. +

APICHATONG WEERASEKATHUS, STILL FROM *TROPICAL MALADY*. 2004. COURTESY KICK THE MACHINE FILMS.

SLOW WARS

Moira Weigel

A FILM BY TSAI MING-LIANG can feel like a test. More specifically, a staring contest. How long can you look? Somewhere into the eleven-minute sequence in *Stray Dogs* (2013), where the protagonist hugs, kisses, and then devours a cabbage with a human face painted on it, I blinked.

Tsai has been developing his glacially slow aesthetic for nearly a quarter century. Born in Kuching, Malaysia, in 1957, to Chinese parents, he moved to Taipei at the age of 20 to attend university—and, the openly gay director has joked, to escape the reputation as a "gigolo" that he was developing in his hometown. He has worked in Taiwan ever since.

Praising his first films, critics immediately identified Tsai as part of the "Taiwanese New Wave" that took off in the late 1980s. Hou Hsiao-hsien, its elder statesman, had become internationally renowned for contemplative portraits of the provincial life set in the past. Tsai, by contrast, has always focused on the contemporary. His setting is usually Taipei, particularly the corners inhabited by its working class—taxi drivers, supermarket cashiers, sidewalk vendors, janitors, construction workers.

Many of his early films take place in parts of the city that have since been developed out of existence. In his first feature, *Rebels of the Neon God* (1992), a trio of teenagers roam the arcades and love hotels of Ximending, the then seedy entertainment district. *What Time Is It There?* (2001) pivots on a chance encounter on a skywalk that was demolished soon after filming. *Goodbye, Dragon Inn* (2003) unfolds during the final screening at a historic movie theater. The camera lingers on these spaces with a mesmeric intensity.

The actor Lee Kang-sheng always plays the lead. Lee incarnates a slightly different character in each film, but all are named Hsiao-kang (小康)—a nickname playing on his real-life first name, but also the expression "little wealth" or "well-being." The phrase signifies modest aspiration; Chinese speakers use it the way Americans used to talk about becoming "middle class." In the glum surroundings in which Tsai sets Hsiao-kang, his name sounds ironic. An elongated sense of time corresponds to stymied upward mobility; Hsiao-kang never gets anywhere.

Stray Dogs epitomizes the deliberate, dilated style that has become Tsai's signature. For two hours, the film follows four characters: a shiftless, alcoholic father (played by Lee); two small children, whom he shepherds through Taipei; and a woman (or trio of women) who also cares for them. The woman is played by three Tsai regulars, decades apart in age: Yang Kuei-mei, Lu Yi-ching, and Chen Shiang-chyi. The scenes themselves are not chronologically continuous.

Shot in static long takes using digital cameras, they're set in a handful of spaces: an abandoned building, roamed by the stray dogs of the title; a shanty that the father has set up for himself and the children to sleep in; a park; a skywalk; a public bathroom where one of the women washes the girl's long hair in the sink and wrings it out under a roaring hand dryer. Not everywhere in this Taipei appears abject. Luminous crane shots show the sand banks of the Tamsui River, gilded by sunset. The father strides as the children scamper along it. The tangled roots of the tropical trees in the park, which the children scramble over, have the Jurassic magnitude of a dreamscape.

The penultimate shot of *Stray Dogs* is both beautiful and punishing. For nearly fourteen minutes, the camera remains motionless, watching the faces of Lee and Chen, the youngest of the three lead actresses, from below. They are bathed in blue light. Around minute eleven, a single tear rolls down her cheek. Thirty seconds later, Lee's character notices, leans forward, and buries his face in her shoulder. They hold that pose until she abruptly switches off the flashlight she had trained on whatever they were staring at and walks off screen.

At last we get the complementary shot: not an eyeline match, from Lee's perspective, but an overhead view, from behind, of the room he has remained in. We are looking from where a projection booth would be, if this room were a movie theater. It is not. It is the foyer of the abandoned building where we previously saw the stray dogs circling.

The floor is littered with trash and rubble, which appears to be chipping off the rain-soaked ceiling.

What have we been watching them watch? On the front wall there is, inexplicably, a mural. It resembles *shan shui* painting, swift black brushstrokes depicting mountains and rivers. The aspect ratio, however, suggests a screen. The rural landscape is like an establishing shot, a postcard from a film that we don't get to see. It's an emblem of the end of cinema: with the image stilled, the theater lies in ruins. The audience assumes its place among the last stray dogs.

Tsai himself has said that he has taken his aesthetic to an extreme that he cannot pursue any further. Presenting *Stray Dogs* at the Venice Film Festival, he announced that this feature would be his last. The statement could be interpreted as bold, canny, or both: the Grand Jury gave Tsai the top prize, the Golden Lion. Tsai reiterated that he was finished making movies at the US premiere at the New York Film Festival. Did he mean it? an interviewer for *Film Comment* asked, on the occasion of the Museum of the Moving Image retrospective of his work seven months later. Tsai equivocated. "If someone invites me, I will consider it." But he said participating in the film market made him feel "powerless."

"I am the kind of person who is afraid of being restrained," Tsai mused. "I feel like my film is always about self-exploration." For now, he does not see how he could take his sensibility further in the cinema. It is easy to see why. With *Stray Dogs*, Tsai seems to have brought the slowness characteristic of contemporary festival films to its limit: stasis.

SINCE THE TURN OF THE MILLENNIUM, there have been few if any coherent national film movements. But internationally, a "slow wave" has swept the festival circuit. Many of the features taking prizes at Cannes, Venice, Berlin, and Toronto fit a profile. Their narratives are nondramatic or nonexistent. The scripts are minimal and repetitive, with little dialogue. They unfold in long takes, captured by still or nearly still cameras. Often the figures in the frame stay still themselves.

These films are not only slow in the sense that some people use that adjective to disparage art cinema out of hand. They are not only plotted and paced differently from Hollywood blockbusters. Festival cinema has been *that* for some time. In a film like *Stray Dogs* it is possible to leave the theater, buy a coffee, check your email, and return to find the actors posed exactly as you left them. This is slowness on a different scale.

Tsai has predecessors in both the film and art worlds. Critics often cite Michelangelo Antonioni as a formative influence. The final scene of *Stray Dogs* echoes the famous final shot of *L'Avventura* (1960). In the film, a wealthy Italian, played by Gabriele Ferzetti, loses his fiancée on a rocky Mediterranean island. With her friend, played by Monica Vitti, he searches for her on the island and then the mainland. The movie unspools into plotlessness, as the two seem to forget why they were looking and fall into a diffident, bitter romance of their own—until Ferzetti has a tryst with a hotel housekeeper. In their final encounter, on the terrace of the hotel, Vitti stands behind Ferzetti, dwarfed by the vertical block of a wall to their right. We watch from behind as she strokes his hair. Her hand falls still on the nape of his neck and stays for nearly half a minute. Critics and filmmakers alike saw this tense, extended gesture as a major innovation, and Antonioni attracted many acolytes.

During the same period, avant-gardists also played with extending time. The "expanded cinema" being made in London and New York during the 1960s experimented with more extreme forms of duration. Andy Warhol called his movie projects "anti-film," because they were essentially unwatchable—"better talked about than seen," he put it. *Empire* (1964) showed eight hours and five minutes of continuous footage of the Empire State Building, projected at sixteen, rather than the standard twenty-four, frames per second. According to legend, Warhol went to great lengths to avoid watching his own anti-films. At the first screening of *Empire*, he got so bored that he snuck out.

The late Chantal Akerman drew together the European New Wave and American experimental film traditions. Having dropped out of film school in Belgium, Akerman traveled to New York in 1970. There she discovered Warhol and other downtown figures like Yvonne Rainer and Michael Snow. Akerman incorporated their techniques into her features, using extremely long takes and fixed cameras to render dead time on-screen. In her most famous film, *Jeanne Dielman, 23 quai du Commerce, 1080 Bruxelles* (1975), the title character is a mother who occasionally does sex work to support herself and her son but spends most of her days on household chores. Akerman sets the camera in front of Jeanne as she chops potatoes, prepares meat, dusts and wipes down chintzy surfaces. The pace is an argument. The nothing we are made to watch happen is this woman's world.

These filmmakers were not the only game in town. Antonioni's chief rival in the international art cinema of the 1960s was Jean-Luc Godard, whose films often involved slapstick comedy and madcap punning; quick, jarring camera movement; and abrupt interruptions on the sound track. The star directors of the New Hollywood of the '70s used rapid editing and violent shifts in tone. Consider *Taxi Driver*. Martin Scorsese's talky, bloody thriller was both a commercial and a festival success; it won the Palme d'Or at Cannes in 1976. Over the past two decades, however, "art" cinema and "slow" cinema have become increasingly synonymous.

From the mid-'90s on, festivals began to consecrate exceptionally slow films. In 1994, Tsai won the Golden Lion at Venice for *Vive L'Amour*, about an empty apartment where the three main characters spend time, alone and with lovers. Tsai intersperses long takes of their interactions inside the apartment with minutes-long shots following them through desolate city spaces. From then on, Tsai became a favorite of the festival circuit. In the same year, the Hungarian director Béla Tarr released his magnum opus, *Sátántangó*, to almost universal critical acclaim. The seven-hour film contains only 150 shots, meaning that the average take lasts nearly three minutes. Many last longer. For five, ten minutes, Tarr lets us watch cows lowing as they leave a barn, or two men walking along a road, whipped by wind and leaves and trash. We see drunken neighbors dance for so long that the eye of the camera itself starts to feel tipsy. Susan Sontag raved about the length and pace, saying she would gladly watch *Sátántangó* once a year for the rest of her life.

Two years later, her *New York Times Magazine* essay "The Decay of Cinema" explained why. Sontag argued that, under assault from Hollywood, the "erotic, ruminative" rituals of filmgoing were dying out. "The reduction of cinema to assaultive images, and the unprincipled manipulation of images (faster and faster cutting) to make them more attention-grabbing, has produced a disincarnated, lightweight cinema that doesn't demand anyone's full attention," Sontag wrote. She joined many of her contemporaries, who fondly recalled the halcyon days of Antonioni and Godard, in lamenting the death of cinema, or at least the dispersal of movies across video and new digital platforms. "Images now appear in any size and on a variety of surfaces: on a screen in a theater, on disco walls and on megascreens hanging above sports arenas," she wrote. "The sheer ubiquity of moving images has steadily undermined the standards people once had both for cinema as art and for cinema as popular entertainment." Figures like Tarr, whose films demanded to be watched on big screens, fulfilled the raison d'être for the cinema: total experience.

There was another, political reason for the enthusiasm for these movies: many of the stars of the slow cinema emerged in the late '90s from countries that, like Tarr's Hungary, had a history of authoritarianism. Watching the films offered "access"—at extravagant length, no less—to otherwise hidden foreign realities. In 1997, the Iranian Abbas Kiarostami took the Palme d'Or for *Taste of Cherry*. Much of it consists of conversations captured by a stationary camera in an automobile. The switch from film stock to digital cameras made it possible for directors to experiment with pace in daring ways. Aleksandr Sokurov's *Russian Ark* (2002) won the Visions Award at the Toronto Film Festival. Shot with a Steadicam, it consists of a single ninety-six-minute take. Sokurov (another Sontag favorite) guides our eyes into and out of rooms populated by hundreds of elaborately costumed cast members. The camera ascends above them, hovering like a ghost; it cants, keels, descends, and finally floats out a door that opens impossibly out onto an ocean.

At this pace, story slips away. While *Russian Ark* is fictional, it is above all a record of a real feat. *Can you believe all those people in those costumes did all those things exactly when they were supposed to?* Jia Zhangke, often called the greatest Chinese director of his generation, also dilated his films with dreamlike long takes that carry fiction to the verge of documentary. *Still Life* won the Golden Lion at Venice in 2006. It opens with a boat voyage down the Yangtze into the town of Fengjie, which will soon be inundated by the construction of the Three Gorges Dam. In scene after wordless scene, a migrant laborer who has returned home to find his estranged wife takes in the doomed landscape. He is played by Jia's cousin, the coal miner Han Sanming. The camera pans, trailing Han's gaze. This act of witness has a moral dimension. Through Jia and his proxy, we take in a world that the contemporary Communist Party has forsaken in the name of progress. But the tone is one of melancholy resignation, not protest.

The difference becomes clear immediately if you watch *Still Life* alongside a more explicitly political documentary made around the same time: *Before the Flood* (2005). Directed by Li Yifan and Yan Yu, *Before the Flood* documents how Fengjie citizens resisted being evicted from their riverfront homes and shops. Through many chaotic scenes, the camera follows citizens making demands at government offices, shrieking in rage, and even physically attacking local officials. Though the film is viscerally disturbing in its own right, the politics on display requires some knowledge of Chinese history and society. The contrast between *Before the Flood* and *Still Life* suggests one of the major reasons why slow cinema plays so well on the international festival circuit. The intense mode of attentiveness it demands can move you, even if you know very little about the particular place you are looking at.

WITH SO MANY OF THESE FILMS winning awards, critics, scholars, and lay cinephiles began to identify a trend. Terms like "slow cinema," "cinema of slowness," and "contemporary contemplative cinema" started circulating at academic film-studies conferences, in journals and festival program notes. Film blogs talked about contemporary contemplative cinema so much that they gave it the shorthand "CCC." Speaking on the "State of Film" at the San Francisco Film Festival in 2003, the French critic and curator Michel Ciment argued that slowness was *the* dominant tendency in contemporary art cinema. The reason why, he said, was simple: Hollywood was speeding up.

Ciment contrasted the average shot length in a series of classical versus contemporary Hollywood films to prove his point: "Where it lasted 7.85 seconds in *Spartacus*, it was only 3.36 seconds long in *Gladiator*, 8.72 seconds in *The Fall of the Roman Empire*, and 2.07 seconds in *Armageddon*." A Bourne movie moved literally twice as fast as a classic James Bond. "Facing this lack of patience and themselves made impatient by the bombardment of sound and image to which they are submitted as TV or cinema spectators," Ciment concluded, "a number of directors have reacted by a cinema of slowness, of contemplation, as if they wanted to live again the sensuous experience of a moment revealed in its authenticity."

A chorus joined Ciment in praising slow cinema as a moral as well as aesthetic triumph. In Britain, a group of young cinephiles started Unspoken Cinema, a blog dedicated to CCC, in 2006; in 2009, a graduate student named Matthew Flanagan published a manifesto in the Danish film journal *16:9* announcing that the "Aesthetic of Slow" had arrived. "In defiant opposition to the quickening of pace in mainstream American cinema, a distinctive narrative form devoted to stillness and contemplation has emerged," he wrote. In the pages of *Sight and Sound*, the British critic Jonathan Romney agreed, suggesting that "the current Slow Cinema might be seen as a response to a bruisingly pragmatic decade in which, post-9/11, the oppressive everyday awareness of life as overwhelmingly political, economic, and ecological would seem to preclude (in the West, at least) any spiritual dimension in art." In an oppressively materialist (and violent) world, slow cinema offered respite, even transcendence.

On festival screens, the slow wave continued to gain mass and momentum. Directors from all over the world were experimenting with languorous pacing and winning recognition for it. In 2010, the Turkish filmmaker Semih Kaplanoglu won the Golden Bear at the Berlin Film Festival for *Honey*, which follows a child searching for his father through the forest at such a slow pace that one critic described it as "a landscape film." That same year, the Thai director Apichatpong Weerasethakul received the Palme d'Or for *Uncle Boonmee Who Can Recall His Past Lives*. Like Weerasethakul's previous films, *Uncle Boonmee* takes place in northeastern Thailand, against the backdrop of the forest whose dark whispers cast a spell; the scenes pass seamlessly between one time and another as the title character is visited by ghosts of loved ones and his own previous incarnations.

There was some backlash. *Sight and Sound* ran an editorial attacking the dominance of slow cinema in its April 2010 issue. "I admire and enjoy a good many of the best films of this kind," the author Nick James allowed, "but I have begun to wonder if maybe some of them now offer an easy life for critics and programmers." The American academic Steven Shaviro followed, charging "old-line cinéphiles" who gushed over CCC with "self-congratulatory" nostalgia. The Slow Wars even spilled over into higher-circulation publications. In April, Dan Kois published a long Riff in the *New York Times Magazine*, complaining that Kelly Reichardt's movies bored him and that watching Andrei Tarkovsky felt like "eating [his] cultural vegetables." In June, Manohla Dargis and A. O. Scott responded with a joint manifesto: "In Defense of the Slow and Boring."

The debate itself was boring. At least, its framing was predictable, pitting the *homme moyen sensuel* versus the last guardians of culture. Meanwhile, slow cinema continued to crawl along. The aesthetic reached American audiences through Terrence Malick, the philosopher turned filmmaker who had returned from a twenty-year hiatus with *The Thin Red Line* (1998). In 2011, Malick won the Palme D'Or for

The Tree of Life. Like *Uncle Boonmee*, the film moves fluidly between different times and even epochs. In a sign that slowness might even one day capture, rather than simply reject, Hollywood, the film was nominated for several Academy Awards.

T HOSE WHO PRAISED SLOW CINEMA as the antidote to Hollywood sounded convincing because they were drawing on such familiar oppositions: contemplation versus distraction, sensuous experience versus technologically driven simulation, grueling authenticity versus facile spectacle, cinema versus "the movies." It was not an accident that enthusiasm for slow film took off at the same time as the Slow Food movement. Both discourses praised slowness as a form of resistance to "globalization" or "Americanization."

The breakneck styles of American-made blockbusters like the Transformers and Fast and the Furious series provided an objective correlative for the exhilarating disorientation of an era when Starbucks started opening hundreds of new stores every year in China, and supply-chain software tracked rare-earth minerals all the way from mines in Congo to iPhones in Shenzhen. With amphetamine-riddled jitteriness, these films cut so fast it was often difficult to tell what was happening. Turn off the sound in a Transformers fight sequence and it looks like an avant-garde experiment in abstract montage. The Bourne franchise presents its global audience with an allegory of their situation. Jason Bourne moves so quickly from one hub of finance to another that the cities collapse into a single kaleidoscope of glass and steel. Often Bourne has no idea whom he is killing or why. He does not even know who he is.

But CCC is not the opposite of Bourne cinema. It is its obverse, the flip side of a single coin. The rise of the slow movement reflected the mutations of old cinematic institutions under the same pressures that were driving Hollywood studios to churn out fast-paced action franchises. It was the festival system that first gave birth to the slow movement. As the festival system has changed, so has the nature and meaning of cinematic slowness.

Historically, festivals have provided institutional space and support—a refuge—for non-Hollywood filmmaking. The European culture ministers who started Venice and Cannes in the 1930s wanted a forum to protect the European film industries from the studios aggressively expanding their distribution networks and conquering foreign audiences. World War II halted their efforts. But after the war, festival organizers set about their purpose with a new zeal—and a new template in geopolitical organizations like the United Nations. Like the UN, the festivals were internationalist in structure, with directors competing as representatives of their home countries. It was through these festivals that a "world cinema" came into being.

In the past, as international cinema culture traveled to new places in search of images, slowness functioned as a kind of delivery mechanism. The festivals served as vehicles for European soft power, exporting Western aesthetic values—including the idea of the "aesthetic" itself, or the belief that art is only art when it inspires disinterested contemplation. The neorealist style pioneered by postwar Italian filmmakers inspired directors around the world.

One of the primary examples of how neorealism could help a filmmaker escape national boundaries is the career of Satyajit Ray. Ray, the most celebrated figure of the "Parallel Cinema" movement that took off in Calcutta in the 1950s and '60s, became a devotee of neorealism after a transformative encounter with the work of Vittorio de Sica. Ray saw de Sica's film *Bicycle Thieves* on a business trip to London. (At the time, Ray was working as a graphic designer.) "All through my stay in London, the lessons of *Bicycle Thieves* and Neorealist cinema stayed with me," he recalled. "*Bicycle Thieves* is a triumphant discovery of the fundamentals of cinema." Ray completed the treatment for *Pather Panchali* (1955) on his return voyage. The first film in his famed "Apu Trilogy," it used foreign protocols to give shape to local material. Like de Sica and his countryman Roberto Rossellini, Ray shot on location using amateur actors and foregrounded scenes of poverty and struggle. Like them, and like the Bengali modernist authors he mined for source material, Ray prized moments of epiphany, acute perceptions, and memories, letting chance occurrences rather than plotted actions drive his films. Based on the great serialized novel of the same title by Bibhutibhushan Bandyopadhyay, *Pather Panchali* takes place in rural West Bengal. It meanders gorgeously, following the daily life of a young boy, Apu, and his sister, Durga. The camera tracks them as they play in their family's courtyard; steal through the forest to snag mangos from a wealthier cousin's yard; watch their stooped and ancient aunt, whose face dissolves into a thousand pleats when she smiles; trail a man who comes through selling candy.

The release of *Pather Panchali* caused confusion in the US. "The most the camera shows us in a rambling and random tour of an Indian village is a baffling mosaic of candid and crude domestic scenes," the *New York Times* film critic Bosley Crowther wrote. "Any picture as loose in structure or as listless in tempo as this one is would barely pass as a 'rough cut' with the editors in Hollywood." But this was the point. Festival audiences were enraptured by Ray's portrait of daily life in a remote setting. Ray won the Palme d'Or in 1955 for the sequel, *Aparajito*, and countless other awards, including an honorary Academy Award for Lifetime Achievement in 1992.

The first success of "world cinema," *Pather Panchali* demonstrated how flexible neorealism could be in conveying "reality" across the world. The "world" in "world cinema" came to signify this style of beautifying semidocumentary slowness, rather than any geographic location. Bollywood and Nollywood productions were watched by millions, if not billions, of people worldwide. But judging by the international festival circuit, they did not count as "world cinema." Their modes of filmmaking were too idiosyncratic, tied too closely to their nations or even cities of origin. Neorealism was better suited for export.

Neorealism was also well suited to a subtle kind of nationalism—or, at least, to telling national stories to an international audience. Many of the greatest "world" films in this style are understated epics. In Bandyopadhyay's bildungsroman, Apu becomes a metonym for modernizing India; adapting the novel in the 1950s, Ray turned the boy into a stand-in for the experiences of the newly independent nation-state. Chen Kaige's *Yellow Earth* (1984) also fit this bill. Shot by Zhang Yimou, Chen's Beijing Film Academy classmate who would go on to become the most famous director in China, *Yellow Earth* takes place during the Civil War of the 1940s. It follows a Communist Party soldier on a long trek through the barren hills of Shaanxi Province to the home of a poor rural family, where he stays while collecting and rewriting local folk songs. Long takes suggest equivalences between the screen, the land, and the body of the young daughter, whose parents are in the process of selling her off. These terse characters become embodiments of history.

Across the straits, Hou Hsiao-hsien's classic film *A City of Sadness* (1989) used slowness to similar effect. The film portrays the painful saga of a large family between 1945 and 1949, chronicling the violence between Communists and Nationalists that preceded the founding of modern Taiwan. Punctuated with long shots of seascapes and lush mountainsides, *A City of Sadness* incarnates the troubled young nation, giving it a wholeness and presence on-screen and inscribing the struggles of the characters within it. In Kiarostami's *Taste of Cherry*, the long takes of the Iranian countryside, seen by car, and brief interviews with representative characters perform a similar function. The tableau they create displays the internal differences of contemporary Iran. These understated histories served a particular function within a festival circuit organized along national lines: they delivered exotic images to metropolitan centers. They edified self-identified intellectual audiences who wanted more than entertainment and were curious about news from abroad.

The slow wave may be what international cinema looks like when it has nowhere new left to go. Slow cinema extends or exaggerates many of the properties of neorealism, enlarging and extending the observational style that allows the landscapes of Ray, Chen, and Hou to come to life on-screen. Yet slow cinema pushes neorealism to the point where its scales tip into something different, a mode that many critics describe as "hyperreal" or "surreal." At the same time, the spaces it takes interest in do not necessarily belong to the nation-state. Its stories do not operate as national histories, and its characters are not representative types.

The great auteurs of slow cinema no longer seem to represent their countries. Many of them belong to more than one. Tsai is a Malaysian living in Taiwan. Like Kiarostami, he gets much of his funding from France. Weerasethakul has raised money for his films in France, the UK, Germany, and the United States, as well as Thailand. Many European directors themselves rely on a mix of transnational film funds. This, too, reflects the vicissitudes of capital, the increasing ease with which it crosses borders. In earlier eras, the funding for "world" films was dispensed at a national level, through culture ministries or government-subsidized TV channels. Today, neoliberal reforms have cut the budgets of such funding bodies. As a result, art filmmakers piece together resources through whatever networks they can.

More and more of them are moving toward alternative institutions that, with looser ties to government and stronger ties to finance capital, are better poised to support them: museums and galleries. In 2006, the Centre Pompidou dedicated a show to Jean-Luc Godard (he had relented after resisting the idea for decades). In the same year, the

Center for Contemporary Culture in Barcelona opened an installation created by Kiarostami and the Spanish auteur Victor Erice: *Correspondences* consisted of a series of opposing screens featuring images of and by each director, and culminated with ten "video letters" that they made and sent each other for the purposes of the exhibition, which traveled on to Madrid and Paris. *Uncle Boonmee* was in fact the final installment of a series of installations called *Primitive* that Weerasethakul made in the Isan region. It includes a video installation—commissioned by Haus der Kunst, Munich, with FACT, Liverpool, and Animate Projects, London—and a short film called *Phantoms of Nabua*, which showed at the BFI Gallery in London.

Tsai, whose feature *Face* (2009) was the first film ever acquired by the Louvre, has continued to make work for museum settings, too. He told *Film Comment* that this was his plan now that he has given up making features. "The movie theater has all kinds of limits, and I think the museum can liberate film," he said. "I hope I can view Taiwan as a starting point to cultivate an audience, by showing films in the museum, making an exhibition, or even making films for the museum." It is no longer Taiwan that supports cinema like Tsai's, or even the international festival, but the non-place of the white box, where the new global super-elite buy up artworks as investments. The kind of intense slowness that becomes unbearable in *Stray Dogs* works well on a loop that a museum spectator can walk by, watch, leave, and return to at will.

In Sontag's and Ciment's critiques of Hollywood, it is the rise of digital filmmaking that has compromised cinema. Yet the aesthetic of slow cinema is digital: Sokurov, Tsai, Jia, and others all use digital cameras. Dissident filmmakers in particular cannot rely on the UN model of the festival to promote their work abroad. They turn to digital distribution platforms. The underground Chinese documentary movement, for instance, has reached a "world" audience through online networks like dGenerate Films. dGenerate, based in Brooklyn, distributes some of Jia's films, and also the celebrated abstract autobiographies of Liu Jiayin, *Oxhide* (2005) and *Oxhide II* (2009), and Wang Jiuliang's slow documentary, *Beijing Besieged by Waste* (2011).

Digital filmmaking, and storing and streaming capabilities, all conspire to disturb the long-standing binary where slow equals art and speed equals commerce; where slow images are aesthetically valuable because they call for contemplation that commercial films do not demand. Slow is a property of many kinds of images. There are many "low" digital objects that Ciment would never claim for art cinema, but that require the same kind of behavior he describes as typical of the "cinema of slowness" he admires. Consider the explosion of found-footage horror films shot with digital cameras, like the Paranormal Activity franchise. These revolve around long swaths of dead time, which require the viewer to actively scan the image, searching for signs of or clues to what is amiss. Consider *Euro Truck Simulator*, the hugely popular video game in which players simulate the driving of a truck in real time. It's like a Kiarostami movie as a video game. Yet it's hard to imagine that Ciment would credit it as an act of resistance.

I F SLOW CINEMA DOES NOT, IN FACT, stand apart from the global economy of digitized images, what does it do? Perhaps it captivates us because it captures a sense of time peculiar to this moment in history—time that grinds on relentlessly while remaining curiously unmoored.

At the turn of the last century, Henri Bergson criticized what he called the "cinematographical" illusion. It was an error, he wrote in *Creative Evolution*, to think of all units of time as equivalent and interchangeable. Instants could not be synthesized mechanically into experience; memory could not be made to move as regularly as the images frozen in the frames of a filmstrip do, once the projector spins them on. In our era of images and information constantly available to be accessed and activated, no one would make the mistake of thinking that it could. Time leaps from place to place. Every moment is pregnant with potential productivity or serendipity; a text message sent from Beijing and received in New York interrupts the here and now. But as a result, the unstructured time that remains seems longer and emptier. For so many of us the future is unknown; the stability of work and the idea of a career belong to the past.

Cinema as a medium came of age under a particular arrangement of leisure and labor. The Fordist economy divided time and space into work and not-work. Whether as mindless entertainment or as high art, movies belonged to the latter. Slow cinema emerged as the industrial economy, and its ways of arranging time and space, began breaking down. Antonioni, so often cited as the first master of CCC, expanded time beyond what narrative required in order to convey the alienation seeping through the cracks of industrial modernity. Antonioni's final film with Monica Vitti, *Red Desert* (1964), shows her coming undone against a Technicolor backdrop of pounding pistons and petrochemical smoke.

Warhol saw still more clearly that the Fordist economy could not hold—that it was giving way to an economy of spectacle. *Empire* turned the duration of the Fordist workday into content for a film. Ninety minutes to two hours had become the standard length for movies, because it was the right amount of time for an audience to spend between punching out and getting to bed in time to rise for work the next morning. By elevating the deadening rhythms and mindless automatisms of factory work into creative principles, Warhol blurred distinctions between process and product, work and play. The visuals not only exceeded the needs of plot. They surpassed or replaced it. At the same time, the leisure the anti-films offered was grueling. They made your body ache with the effort of sitting and watching, just as you might ache after hours on an assembly line.

Like Warhol, Chantal Akerman focused on forms of work the Fordist economy did not account for. Akerman always refused to call herself a feminist filmmaker, but in retrospect it is impossible not to read the interminable scenes of housework in *Jeanne Dielman* as being in conversation with the Wages for Housework movement. *Jeanne Dielman* demands that the work its protagonist does be recognized as such. Akerman also resembled Warhol in that she foregrounded the relationship between her life and her art—between the forms of female labor that her films depicted and her own creative process. It is as if she were following a late-capitalist variation on Flaubert's famous dictum, "Be regular and orderly in your life like a bourgeois, so that you may be violent and original in your work." Her later films like *Là-bas* (2006) and even her final film, *No Home Movie* (2015), reveals the methodical, repetitive, even obsessive elements of her process. She alludes to her own compulsion to shut herself indoors, in private spaces, to get her work done.

Warhol emphasized that in the economy where everyone would be famous for fifteen minutes, producing and consuming spectacle, and above all producing *oneself* as a spectacle, could become a full-time job. ("I suppose I have a really loose interpretation of 'work,'" he quipped in *The Philosophy of Andy Warhol*, "because I think that just being alive is so much work at something you don't always want to do.") Akerman drew attention to work that had long gone unseen or unrecognized. Both used a grinding kind of temporality to convey their insights: that days did not divide so cleanly as classical cinema had supposed. Time in their films opens into one often-deadening continuum, which rarely leads to the development of anything like story. Perhaps it is no accident that both of these filmmakers were queer—as is Weerasthakul, as is Tsai. The sexual energies that their films exude can be intoxicating, but they do not culminate in long-term couplings the way Hollywood romances do. From the perspective of a bourgeois economy, their eroticism is not productive.

Today the Fordist paradigms whose fraying edges the slow cinema of the 1960s and '70s pointed to have definitively broken down. The slow cinema of the 2010s excels at depicting the dead time that dominates so many lives under neoliberalism, when occasional and precarious labor is increasingly the norm. In 2003, Ciment spoke of the difference between Hollywood's cinema of "distraction" versus an art cinema of "contemplation." Yet if CCC demonstrates anything, it is that distraction and contemplation, or attentiveness, produce each other. Shots that last a quarter-hour force their viewers to cycle between attention and distraction, in a negative feedback loop that reverses itself several times over.

In interviews, Béla Tarr described his final film, *The Turin Horse*, as aiming to depict "the heaviness of human existence." "We didn't want to talk about mortality or any such general thing," Tarr told *Cineuropa* in 2011. "We just wanted to see how difficult and terrible it is when every day you have to go to the well and bring the water, in summer, in winter. . . . All the time." The long takes showing the horse capture the heaviness of its body and the strain of the work it does. The camera fixes on its plodding, sinewy limbs and on the tensed and hunched back of its owner, his cold-chapped hands clenching the reins, the wind whipping the horse's mane and kicking up dust we can almost feel stinging our eyes. Sometimes a misstep by the animal tugs his arms, making him lurch forward. The weight of all this life wasted doing grunt work accumulates as the film wears on.

Jia, too, is an expert in depicting how the days of many of his characters dissipate. We see miners and migrant laborers sleeping on a boat en route to Fengjie, playing cards and lounging long after they have docked. But we see the epiphanies that such dead time can produce, too. A wandering glance can open up a spectacular vista of the river. The migrant workers in his film *The World* (2004) spend their downtime fiddling with their cell phones; Jia periodically lets animations based on their messages take over the screen, as if the drabness of their lives could suddenly be overcome by the force of their imagination and desires. In one surreal scene in *Still Life*, a brutalist tower alongside the Yangtze suddenly shakes free of its foundations. In a stunning moment of metamorphosis, it turns into a rocket and takes off.

Perhaps more than any other director, Tsai foregrounds the highly irregular rhythms that shape the lives of those who work on the low end of the Bourne economy. All the different versions of Hsiao-kang whom Lee Kang-sheng has incarnated over the decades have shit jobs that involve endless waiting. They drive taxis or hawk knockoff watches on overpasses. Though they peruse stalls of bootlegged DVDs or jangling electronic malls aimlessly, their dead time also has its upsides. In many films, characters spend long stretches of time cruising; aimlessness becomes electrified with a diffuse sexual energy. In many shots in *Goodbye Dragon Inn*, we follow a female cleaner with a lame leg lugging buckets of water up the stairs of the dilapidated movie theater, water sloshing onto the grubby floor. But we also see men taking advantage of the nearly empty screening to flirt. Tsai can puncture a dreary scene with a deadpan sense of humor. In *What Time Is It There?*, a corpulent man trails Hsiao-kang through a dingy electronics mall where he is shopping for a new watch. When Hsiao-kang goes to a public bathroom, the stranger springs out of one of the stalls. Pants down, he holds a large clock over his groin. The jammed second hand bounces back and forth, between the 5 and the 10, beckoning. Neither of them says a word.

Stray Dogs constantly returns to scenes of Hsiao-kang doing occasional work, or waiting to work, or gobbling down street food in between. His main gig seems to be standing in a poncho under pelting rain, holding a sign that advertises a sunny new real estate development. Despite the weather, and the rush and splatter of the passing cars, he remains frozen, the support for an image, a human advertisement for a drier, warmer place. In one of these scenes, Hsiao-kang bursts into song; he sings of a 13th-century hero as tears stream down his cheeks. The tune is at once plaintive and ironic; against the monotony of the passing cars, it feels uplifting because it at least gives us something to pay attention to. In another scene, Hsiao-kang suddenly throws the sign to the ground and stamps on it in blind rage. It is the accumulation of time that gives both bursts of emotion their force.

Tsai has made one feature-length film since *Stray Dogs*. *Journey to the West* is a documentary of a performance project that comments on the state of world cinema. The title refers to the classic Buddhist epic but also ironically alludes to Tsai's status as an Asian world filmmaker, who must constantly make work to appeal to juries and audiences abroad. In *Journey to the West*, Lee Kang-sheng appears in the saffron robes of a monk. He is on a street in Marseille. He performs a ritual, walking as slowly as he can, so slowly that his movement is almost imperceptible. In ninety minutes, he may cross a block or two. His gaze remains fixed steadfastly on the ground. Some passersby stare; some pass, without casting a glance his way. Though I have tried many times, I have never managed to watch all of it.

Is this how cinema transcends itself? In the age of online streaming, the spectator can move and the image stays fixed; if this surfeit creates a kind of monotony, it means that monotony is also always there to be summoned. In the end, *Journey to the West* turns boredom into a kind of meditation. The *mise en abyme*, as we watch strangers watch Lee watch nothing, suggests that digital images have become the grounds of our mobile existence. Seen or unseen, they are the stream we move on. +

PEMA RINZIN, *AUSPICIOUS DREAM 2 (LEFT PANEL)*. 2013, SUMI INK, GOLD, STONE PIGMENT ON WOOD, 36 × 48".
COURTESY JOSHUA LINER GALLERY.

FOUR POEMS

Sophie Robinson

I HATE FLOWERS

all i want is sinking ships
all i want is ships under water
trains under water

cars dropped from ships into water
trains carriage by carriage like links
of sausage dragging each other under

transport is so playful without weight
or purpose—metal bubbled laughter
a whole sea of metal and salt

i don't want to be taken anywhere
i want the traffic to stay still
i want the future lost & rusted

all i want is everything
underwater forever rendered
in scum

i want everything looking
like a shitty picture
of what it used to be

IDK

yesterday I ordered a scoop
of each of the three flavours
of ice cream they had
& they brought me nine:
three shining bowls
w/three shining scoops
of each.

today I bounced home
in a storm found
a tenner blowing on the floor
& then another
so thin the queen
was almost gone.
I guess I'm still
Getting used to the art
of letting things
glow—

it can't last forever.
feeling like this.

IF I COULD KILL MY FREAKS

to choose to spend your nasty
sour little days with anyone
or chew them out alone to burst
as rancid bubbles through the neon
straw of your perfection: it slackens
perspective to even think it—makes
my wrists sweat valium
yellow through themselves
& the shirt & the jumper & the coat.
nothing stops that rancid branching
of my body out west & east
of itself to draw you in *as though i care*
which way you coil your hose—!

you could take a slice of my luv
& not want for weeks
but i've eaten the whole & blobby quiche—

> *"sophie please do a better job of yourself!*
> something has been sleeping
> on your ruins & it barks & whines
> all night. we are all very tired.
> take 4x painkillers
> & turn off the light"

WHERE THE HEART IS STREAMING

there are places in which the mind thrives like plankton, where jobs
are easy to come by & every apartment overlooks the park, where
the funeral has barely started & the heart is a mist that rises & clears
like a browser & streaming faster—a gapless surface of fake solids

& there are places in which love reproduces itself like a lizard's tail, heeds
to no alarm or database. places where the sun rises like a fat cunt
glowing in the sky. places where the rats don't race but rat out
their days in a waterlogged stupor. places you can dive into from a height

there are places where a heart is megashared & its kitchens always full
of foods. where babies name themselves. a place you cannot unknow
& in some place from the past there is a bucket doubling as a womb, full
of infant newts & frogspawn. in some place you cannot know is you

full to the brim with ungendered yearning. & there are places that smell
of honey and decay, places where mistakes can be undone by pressing
a sequence of two or three keys. places where the language flows uncoded,
where everybody understands each other. there are places where people

burn money to keep warm, places where every shop window is broken & blood
makes patterns on the walls. there are places where every building looks
the same & nothing can be bought or sold. there are places through which
a tall fence runs with holes too small to kiss your opposite number

& there are places in which each citizen is tattooed, head to toe, with the face
and body of another citizen & everybody takes to the lakes naked, places
where public transport is free & police tip their hats to beggars on the streets
& nobody dies. there are places where the dead rise from their graves

& avenge the living, places where the dead turn into doves just to peck
themselves dead again. there are places in which bleeding takes the place
of talking, places with water in place of mirrors, with eyes instead of cameras,
patches of pure darkness on a google map, places you can't arrive or leave

& there are places in which the lives of happy and boring people unfold
day after day, where nobody writes anything down & nobody suffers
from the damp & cold. there are places you have been & will
never go again, where the yearning to visit stands in for the visiting

as though you could trick yourself out of death or labour for a second
go at being free. there are places where the moon is god-blocked into
a pinprick, & places where it largens & honeys, places night never falls
& the citizens sleep with snakes across their eyes to block the light

& the heart itself a snake knotted into a place we can never see or fathom
a stupid fist raised in protest, shrinking by the minute, longing to be dropped
in steaming water, to expand to the size of a glass like a hybrid tea rose sewn
together in a factory in bangladesh & sold for eight hundred times its worth

& the workers streaming utopia their bodies dropping from the walls all night

JORDAN KASEY
May 27th-June 26th, 2016
SIGNAL | ssiiggnnaall.com

ASA
NISI
MASA

ACE HOTEL
New Orleans Pittsburgh Los Angeles London
Palm Springs New York Portland Seattle

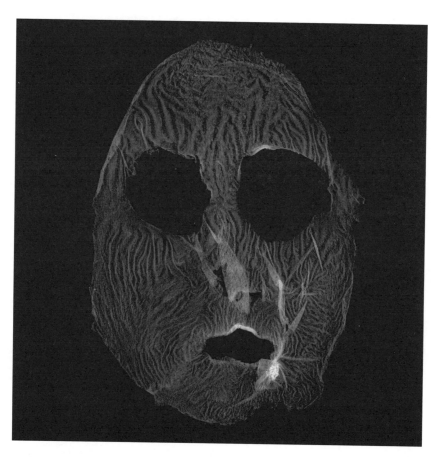

BARBARA ASTMAN, *I AS ARTIFACT #12*. 2011, DIGITAL PRINT ON ARCHIVAL PAPER, 35 × 35".
COURTESY OF THE ARTIST AND THE CORKIN GALLERY, TORONTO.

CALLS

Masande Ntshanga

T HERE WAS A SPIRIT Pa used to ask me about when we were starved. "When were you born?" he'd say.

"I don't know."

"You can ask it?" he'd tell me, and then he'd wave his hand around in the dark.

I'd shake my head.

"You don't believe?"

"I can't see it," I'd say.

Then he'd bang out tobacco from his pipe against the headboard and get up. Pa would look out the window, then, and I often fell asleep with him standing there.

T HE FIRST TIME PA put a hand to his side was while driving us back from a call; with his other hand he reached for my head and peeled me off my seat. The steel door felt cold as it caught the small of my back and his bottle spun to a stop between us, slipping into a groove rusting on the truck bed. His ceiling had cracked the previous year, and often the wind peeled the tape we used to seal it. Now the wind seeped in through the cracks and heaved in warm pellets of rain. Pa used to say each ping reminded him of a god without favor. Other times he would say there was a creature he could feel was perched above us, one spitting marrow into a small cage.

He rolled down his window and spat, too, that night.

"Keep it from me," he said and patted his side. "I'm burning."

I nodded and went back to my seat.

Then we drove the rest of the way to the boxes in silence.

I looked out the window and Pa bottomed his bottle before we reached home.

Inside our box, I latched the door, loosened his belt, and undid his boots. I blew out the paraffin lamp, and in the day that followed, I watched him as he lay shackled on his mattress. He said the sweat ran over his body like ball bearings, that night, and I moved away from the hand he stretched out toward me. In the morning, Pa rose to his feet again, but his head was leant crooked. It inched toward the ground as if to listen to a grave, he said.

I T WAS MONDAY and I was thinking of him. I shifted into second and U-turned across the first traffic island in Rosebank. Then I ran a red light and cut into Main and Church Streets.

My father.

Pa and I never used to talk on our drives home. We used to work on the routine he'd set up between us. I was a boy. I had to offer him his whiskey and he'd wave me away.

Pa never needed words to offer me his meaning. He had only to sit down with his neck stiff, and I remember his long face, how his eyes would bolt down on the road whenever he took the wheel, and how I used to think he was dead, at times, when the two of us left the city limits and the wheels on the van would crunch the gravel on the narrow tracks. I remember how his tears would soak into his beard.

It was late that Monday, and taking the bend, I shifted back down to first.

Then I took a breath and shook him out of my head.

My call was a four-room brick face with a man down. His blood hadn't drained down to his ankles yet, but I had to rush in order to find out what remained. He lay in a small building, they'd told me, and its yellow light was spilled on a yard a block ahead.

I shifted the van back up to second before I hit the brakes and clutched for a hump. Then I took it down to first, again, for the incline, and that's when I heard them.

Often, our calls would arrive this way. First we had to drive up to where a body was laid down, and then we had to hear the sound of its women.

Often, they wailed.

Once, when it was just me and Pa, it was laughter that surrounded a house.

Outside the yard, I shifted down to neutral and left the van on idle.

Then I thought of my father. Pa taught me everything I knew about calls.

"This is a call we're on," he used to say.

The job used to come easy to men like him. Pa had been drafted for a post working with EMS recruits: our work at the boxes was still in phase one, back then, and it hadn't been emptied of its funds. Healers were settled into terms with the clinics. This was during the first wave of sleepers in the city, and Pa liked to take me with him on the late-night rides. We used to take the commuter line in and drive back out with the hospital men. He'd touch my shoulder whenever he needed a whiskey. The roads we got on were bumpy, then, and farther out from the city. Often they made Pa sick, and sickness turned him churlish. I often heard the bottle rattle inside his cooler box as it broke his needle kit. Pa never used the needle kits.

"That's your last one, now," he used to say.

Then I'd take my last sip and cap his bottle. I'd push his whiskey back in the cooler.

"It's right you bring some fear to it," he'd say, and I always nodded when he spoke.

OUTSIDE THE YARD, I shook him out of my head, again. Then I pulled the key to kill the engine. My call had a set of bars cast over its door. Its light streamed through the windows and each square pulled a slat of yellow over the yard. It was a sunken home. It had a small wire fence and the grass was wilted. There was a cement walkway that led up to a red stoop and on top of it lay two plastic chairs: one turned over on its side. It was a pink house, flanked by two arid plots, and I could hear its women weeping inside.

My phone hummed on the passenger seat.

It was a call from my dispatcher, and I turned it over to hide its face against my thigh. I didn't want to speak to Leonard, but I knew he wouldn't stop calling me about the side. I waited for it to shake again. Then I turned it over to look at what he'd sent.

"Five hundred."

That was his offer.

Earlier that night, he'd called me up for the side when I'd taken out the van.

"Cue me your location," he'd said.

"I'm on the road, Leonard. I'm two blocks down from the site."

Then he'd gone quiet. Leonard liked to be called Larry on call nights.

"Good," he said. "Now listen."

I listened. He pressed the phone against his bulk and moved. Leonard shifted his feet across the floor and I could tell he was searching his box for quiet.

"Listen," he said. "They've found a girl there."

He dropped his voice to a whisper. On Leonard, a whisper came out in hisses, but he was a man who felt favored by them. He didn't like the men he shared his box with, he said.

Our dispatch office, where Larry made his calls, was housed in a shipping container in a township on our west coast. The settlement was reported as modest in our city records, which meant that privacy was a thing its people only heard rumors about.

The boxes were rent-fixed and corrugated to streamline insulation, Leonard said, and often, he'd take a chair out to smoke a cigarette on the gravel patch outside his own, sunning himself while he joked about the closeness of our toilets and the likelihood of illness.

The boxes were shanties, each fitted into rows that made up one of the city's many squatter-camp holds, and most of us could never tell if Leonard meant the pride he displayed at living in one—inside a plywood shack, a zinc four-corner, or the new shipping containers that were stolen and sold to us from the south harbor—as a method of injuring our own. Our dispatcher often had a grin he wouldn't drop whenever he stepped out of a box.

I remembered the first time I signed up with him. He'd had the four of us stand outside his box for an hour before he swung his arms up and laughed. Then he'd pointed us to a van that sat on cinder blocks across the way, rusting at a crooked angle under the sun.

It was all that remained of the hospital men, he said. Then he read our call sheets back to us and we each left feeling better than we had the previous morning. It had excited us, in the end, that a man in our business could carry on him the smell of meat.

"Larry," I said. "I'm not doing any more sides. I've been put on medicine."

"I know, just hear me out. This is an open option. You touch her or you don't. The deal's going for five hundred. That's all I'm saying."

"Five hundred?"

"Five hundred."

I heard him trap his bad cough. Leonard had a bad cough he liked to trap inside his chest. It burnt him before he'd lay a fist on his ribs to wheeze it out.

"Just think it over," he said.

"I don't think I will, Larry."

"I don't think I will, Larry," he said.

I could see him throwing his arms up in his box, the sweat beads tracking down his nose as he heated up. That was good. It left me satisfied to think of Leonard that way.

I had my doors locked and my windows rolled. The yellow light from the call fell on my hood as I waited in the car. From behind the wheel, I could see birds slicing across the pane.

Then I took a moment to think about the side.

Most of us called them *sides* from how we'd find them, but just as often, it was to keep the men from thinking of their names. Most of the girls we found were children, but we could never tell when we'd come across one, or how they'd come to find the floor of a house. Most times, all we could do was knock on a door and wait.

"It's all good luck," Leonard would say. "If you don't touch this girl, you'd have to walk out and fill your head with whatever you're leaving her to."

"You could leave her to rest."

"You could leave her to rest," he'd say. "Not even on her feet. Listen to yourself."

I never knew what to tell him. Often, we'd find the sides in worse shape than we did their calls. It didn't help to tell a house to let them go, either, since none of them ever did.

"Let them go where?" they'd say, and I never answered.

Instead, I always wondered what Leonard would tell them.

If Pa lived, he'd be halfway down the length of his bottle. It set him drinking, to be sent out on calls. Pa needed a big fog in his head to bring his hands to use, and he couldn't do the work they gave him when his head was clear. He wasn't much good at it, he used to say.

Maybe I'd see him too, I thought, darting under their lights. Outside, the ravens circled a narrow berth around the roof of the house, keeping a close vigil on where the tiles had been set to hold up the vane. I couldn't tell if it creaked under their cries or not, but the tin looked old to me, like it leaned on something crooked. Maybe it had a burden on its side like Pa.

I kept my eyes up. One of the birds came down to claw at my hood. I watched her climb up the van and open her beak, and the two of us stared before she flew back when I knocked on the dash.

Then I stepped out for a smoke. Down the road I could see the railway line, and it gave me thoughts of leaving, to look at an old house like that. I was put on medicine, I thought. Maybe work won't take away what's left of me.

Inside the van, I stuck my hand in the dash. I found an empty bottle, a nip standing on its head at the back of the hole. I'd been off bottles since I started on my meds; I couldn't tell if I missed them or not. They took away my time, but left a sweet taste in my smokes.

I felt for my bag. Pa's the one who'd taught me how to tie a bag. He said to find loam and to break the loam with ivy. Pa could fill up with lessons for me on a drive. He didn't mind the hospital men, he said. It kept the hospital men quiet, and each man could keep an eye out on the road. None of them could figure Pa from his work. It kept him drinking, when he didn't have a word to spare. I still thought about him.

I closed my dash and found my amulet. I always let it dangle down my front. It was a small disc, the size of a rand, and I let it hang down from a knot of twine.

The air was warm. Daylight heated the roads leading down from the mountain, raising the smell of tar that hung over their yard. My call had a broken gate. The bottom wire was trapped, and it scraped out runnels on the soil when I pushed it. I thought about how that gate felt like an omen. I remembered Pa's large hands on my shoulders, the smell of whiskey on my skin. My father told me never to run when he took me on calls. I knocked twice on their door. Then turned around to cast an eye over my van.

Often on the road I saw the night sky rising in black bars between their houses, and I heard the voices of their women push themselves up against the panes. Tomorrow night would mark the start of another set of calls being taken down at the boxes, which would bring with it more roads, and I would knock on their doors until none of us were left.

T HE CRIES STOPPED and a woman arrived to work on the latch. On the threshold, she was wearing a black tunic, the cloth fitting her like a loose tube.

"We didn't know you were here."

"It's all right," I said. "How long's he been down?"

"It's been a day, sir. We brought him in from the clinic."

I nodded and watched as she pulled a key from her chain.

"Where is he?"

"The kitchen, sir."

"You don't want to bury this man?" I said. "You've decided this?"

"Please, sir," she smiled and unlocked the gate. "Could you follow me?"

I followed her.

We walked into a narrow hall. The house was sunk under the smell of damp wood and paraffin fire; there was a gray carpet leading up to the kitchen, and the living room was small, crowded with couches kept inside cracked plastic sheets.

"I'm Wezile," she said, and I nodded. I never gave my name out on calls.

"The largest space we have is the kitchen."

Locking the door, she apologized and returned to my side.

"Everything has been cleared for you."

Her head was hung low, and I could see where her sallow skin had started to crease. Her eyes fell in crests at the edges of her face, but each orb was still brilliant from her tears.

"On Monday, Mister started complaining of a pain in his chest. He woke up screaming in his bed, sir, and he told us he was being stabbed."

I nodded.

"How many of you live here?"

"Four," she said.

Her fingers rose over her shoulder as she led me down the hall toward the kitchen, which was lit up at the far end of the passage.

I couldn't see the others, but there was a window hung on the opposite wall. It had no curtains, and as we drew close, a raven swooped past the pane.

"What does he do for work?"

"Mister drives a truck from Durban, sir. He has his job with petroleum."

We walked into the kitchen and she pointed to the others. They were all dressed in the same tunic, kneeling on the lino and crouching around the body.

I stood at the door. I could see the chest on the man, but not Leonard's side.

"The healer is here," Wezile said, and each of them turned, reaching up to greet me.

"I need you to find something to cover that window with," I said from the door. "Then I need you to bring me two buckets. Fill only the one with water."

"Yes, sir."

Wezile left, and when she returned she used a white tablecloth to drape the kitchen window. She opened the cabinets below the sink and pulled out two buckets; one of them was blue and the other was silver. I watched her let the water drum against the plastic base, which left the rest of us standing behind her in silence.

I decided to walk in and shake their hands. Even though they offered me their names, I wouldn't keep them. I was on a call. On a call, one name meant more than enough.

The man lay on his back and the women parted as I drew close.

He was dressed up. They'd fitted him inside a gray suit with a silk tie. His feet were covered in navy socks, and each foot was tied under a polished brogue. The costume didn't surprise me. Most of the calls we got had trouble separating our work from a burial. They wanted this man on his feet but had prepared him for a casket. I knew it from the nights I used to go on the road with Pa. It's only the fear of a house, he used to say.

I dropped my bag and placed a hand over his chin. His breath felt light on my fingers.

Then I asked Wezile for salt.

Uncapping the blue lid on her shaker, I poured two handfuls into the bucket. Then I stirred it in with my hand, feeling the sharp plastic ridges raised at the bottom. My plastic bag lay slumped by my side. I used my free hand to undo its knot and dug my fingers into the loam, sifting it for ivy. I was on my knees when I turned back to face him.

My call looked comatose.

His skin was peeling off his cheeks and his eyes were sunken under the brow. His nose was narrow, the mouth below it pursed, and even at his age, which I thought of as 55, his frame was large but sinewy. He had taut neck muscles and his hands were upturned at his sides. Each was the size of a child's boxing mitt.

I looked up again.

"Did this man beat any of you?"

They were quiet. I flicked the water off my fingers and steadied the bucket.

"Not often," Wezile said.

I nodded. It was better if a house offered us the truth. That's what Pa used to say. I still remembered the nights he'd take me on bad calls. My father always left a body cold if the house wasn't dealing him straight. There wasn't much of a point to it, he'd say.

I undid the man's tie. It was folded tight, and I had to turn the ribbon over his neck to push his collar open. Then I started on the buttons.

"Did he live inside?"

"Mostly, sir. We have another room at the back."

Wezile shuffled to my side and I thought of Leonard again.

"Sir, could I get you something to drink?"

I shook my head as she got to her feet.

I thought I could hear her bones creak over the lino.

On the floor, I parted the man's gray lapels and broke open the rest of his buttons. I felt my patience slipping. On my knees, I watched as the buttons scattered and sank into the crevices below the cabinets. I wanted them to look for each of those pellets after I left. They'd find them sitting behind spiderwebs clutching half-eaten husks, I thought, and maybe then they'd stop to consider this man's prey.

"I need you to bring me a blade."

Wezile nodded and left the kitchen. I turned back to the others.

"You don't keep any Bibles here?"

They stared at me before the tallest one nodded. She was thin and looked to be the youngest. Her skin was firm and as sallow as the first's. I told her to come closer.

"I need you to take those out of the house," I said to the rest. "Take the crosses, too."

I turned back to the girl.

"You'll have to touch him. I need you to open his mouth."

The girl nodded and knelt down; straddling his head with her knees, she pried his mouth open and kneaded him in both cheeks to keep his jaws split. I could tell she'd lost any feeling she might've once held for him.

I watched her work. The girl's hands were steady, and she only jumped when the first bird clattered its beak against the window. I also looked up then. It wouldn't be long until they came at the pane like hail.

"Don't be afraid," I said. "They'll leave when we're done."

I sat back. I could feel the itch of the ivy climbing up my fingers. It formed a red rash around my fist and I pushed my hand back in the bag until it was covered with loam. Then I shook my amulet out of my shirt and pulled my fist out again, full of soil, and poured the loam over each of his eyes. Then I filled up his mouth.

I now needed to cut him, but Wezile wasn't around.

"You can let go of him," I said. "I need you to take off his socks."

The girl undid his laces as I turned to scan the kitchen for knives. I was at the counter when Wezile walked back in and handed me a pack of razors. I took one before we gathered around the call. The girl knelt down. Wezile stepped a foot away from us.

"How many of you did he rape?" I asked.

They didn't answer, and I turned back to the girl.

"It was all of us," she said.

I nodded. Then, for a reason I couldn't tell, the action made me relent. I decided to ask her for her name. She told me it was Lindiwe, and there was a lull as I took it in. Then Wezile walked to the counter and uncrossed her arms.

"Will he be good now?"

I didn't answer. They always asked me this, and I never told them. I never believed I could change what a call was, and I never came back to find out if I did. I only had the words I'd once heard Pa use on a house.

"I'll drain him," I said. "Then I'll take on what's inside him."

Wezile moved back with the girl. I took off my amulet and pressed it down on his chest. Keeping the disk in place, I used the blade to trace a small circle around the rim. The man's blood seeped and I peeled off his skin. Then I leaned forward to remove the charm.

"You've hidden her," I said.

The two of them remained silent, but each stood with their faces turned toward me.

"Sir, we had no other choice."

Wezile paced across the kitchen and stopped.

"We didn't know if we had your help."

I stood up and held my amulet; Lindiwe turned her face down and shook her head.

"We should let him rot, sisi. This is costing us a fortune. We should use this money on the house. We don't have a guarantee he'll change."

"This man is a healer, Lindiwe. You must trust in his work."

"Healer? He won't trust it himself, sisi. He tells us of draining. What is draining?"

The girl wasn't wrong, but Wezile stood unmoved. The elder wanted to know if I could turn their man into a saint, and I couldn't. Instead, I shrugged, feeling tired for each of us.

"He'll walk," I said. "Now I need you to tell me where you've hidden the child."

"She's in the flat, sir."

I waited for more, but both of them were still. I could tell the other two with the crosses wouldn't return.

"Well, I want to see her," I said.

"Please, sir. We can bring her after."

I shook my head.

"She's in the bathtub," Lindiwe said. "I carried her in last night."

We headed for the bath. Lindiwe led us down the hall and we entered the last door before the lounge, where the light switch wouldn't turn, gluing us to the frame.

I could make out the child's limbs. Her right arm and leg were slung over the rim and there was no scent inside, only the faint smell of old detergent. Her head was rolled back with its top against the wall, and she stared open-mouthed at a place beyond the ceiling, looking older, I thought, than what Leonard had sent me for.

HEAVED HER UP. Taking her by the underarms, I draped her over my shoulder and wedged myself between the women. Then I started down the hallway, feeling leaden in all my limbs.

"The man said you would take five hundred for her," Wezile said, but I didn't answer.

"Please, sir, don't let this stop you."

"It won't stop me," I said. I laid the girl down on the floor.

"We also want this child to live," she said.

I never knew if any of them did.

I once asked Pa why he had a house take away its Bibles when they called for him, but he never answered me. He only took me by the hand and led me out to the back of our box, where he handed me his coat and laid himself out on the soil. Then he told me he was a call and that I had to work on him.

I did.

The late sun fell flat on my back as I took out the bag. It drew small shadows that deepened the grooves in his neck, and I stuck my tongue out to think. I didn't nick him in the vein. Pa grew his nostrils, and I was almost done with him when he laughed.

He reached into his shirt and pulled out his amulet with the string. Then he reached in again and pulled out a crucifix.

I tried to work through my anger.

"What's it for?" I asked, but he only laughed.

Then he got up and beat the dust from his coat.

We were both inside when he told me none of them knew.

THE GIRL'S BRAIDS HAD FALLEN in a tangled web around her head, and I could see they hadn't dressed her. She was in a threadbare nightgown and its white flaps were open at the sides, revealing her naked body, which lay unmarked on the kitchen floor. My call must've used his hands, I thought. Then I searched her neck and found her pulse.

This came as part of the job.

Dispatchers kept dropping their ages to bait us out on calls. It was an old practice; sides meant a double cinch for men who worked dispatch, but depending on their age, it made the job tough for a man on the road. We got sick from taking on old sides.

I told Wezile I'd take her water, and when she returned, she carried a yellow enamel cup, brimming and dented around the lip, and set it shaking at my side.

"Sir, maybe I could go get you the money now?"

"No. I need you to see if this works."

"Won't it?"

I shrugged.

The water wasn't too cold. I drained the cup and went over to the girl. Pulling the saltwater bucket toward me, I dipped and rinsed both hands before I arranged her head next to the man's. How many times had he arranged them just this way, I thought, the head of a predator along its prey. Then I started on her with the loam. I went over each of her eyes before filling up her mouth. Then Wezile handed me a fresh blade, and I placed the disk on her chest. Her skin was soft, and it didn't take much to peel a piece off.

I took some of her with me to the call. On my knees, I pushed the amulet back inside his wound and touched him on the crown. I cupped the top of his skull with my fingertips and eased my hand behind the back of his head, which, even shaved, felt hefty on my palm.

Then I breathed twice and he jumped.

The ebb took him whole, lifting his back in an arch before planting his feet on the floor. I pushed my other palm under his back, and that took what was left of me. It didn't take long before I passed out, kneeling crooked at the sides of his head.

Opening my eyes, again, I saw him touch back on the floor. I'd seen too many men fall on their backs, I thought, and I turned his head over, spilling the soil in a slush out of his mouth. The ravens cawed outside, and my call began to choke. He doubled over on his side and gripped his stomach, filling back into what should've been left a corpse.

I thought of that. Maybe Pa took me out on too many calls.

They used to cover my eyes when my father started raising.

I used to stand waist-high against the women inside a house, and before he'd lay his hands on a call, he'd tell them to cup a palm over my eyes. I knew my father's men from their smell before I ever saw them jumping off their floors. It was a smell I knew. It pushed into the room and filled me with a picture of home. I remembered the rain, and how we used to stalk each other's backyards for worms. Our boxes had no wires back then, and when the gas hissed low, we'd stoke a fire and lay it out on the hearth. The firewood would take on the form of charred bones, and underneath it, below sheets of rusted zinc, we'd discover the worms and their holes. Later, when I rode with Pa on his calls, I could remember those days. I could remember the smell that came with the burden of winter.

It smelled of wet ash.

The scent filled the room, and Wezile walked over with water for the call. I motioned for her to keep her distance, but only the young one listened; she caught her elder by the shoulders and drew her back, keeping them stood in place by the counter.

Then I turned and took another look at him.

Their choking often came with the smell. Calls would convulse before they fell silent again, at which point they'd fall into the slumber of a stone. It was what I treasured most about the road. We never got to see these men walking inside their homes.

I bent down and held his head. Then I rinsed the rest of the soil from him by cupping saltwater and splashing it inside his mouth. On waking up, he'd feel as good as buried. The thirst would make his skin feel tender but taut, and his meat would clutch hard against the bone.

I looked up again.

"Wezile, I'll need you to bring me the money now," I said.

"Of course, sir."

"The birds are gone," Lindiwe said when Wezile left. She looked up to study the tablecloth, keeping her eyes strayed far from the girl.

"They were here for Vuyani," I told her.

I didn't know why I'd taken on his name, but that was what most of us would tell them. The truth was that the ravens had only started perching on their houses a year ago. There were reports that they'd been drawn to the cape by a change in climate, and others that pinned it to the city's rise in carrion. I could never tell. It seemed, on most days, that it was all of us who were headed toward waste.

Lindiwe paused and faced down again.

"This is not a good thing we did," she said. "I can tell from how you work you don't think it's a good thing."

I shrugged. I arranged the girl's braids on the side of her face and spread the roots of her hair to reveal her crown. I was back on my knees, again, and I shuffled closer to her.

"I brought her in last night," Lindiwe said. "Sisi thinks I don't know what he is, but I know. I knew when I came here. Maybe the others don't."

I asked her about them.

"They've gone to pray with Tatu'Mthembu, sir. He's a churchman down the road from here. That's where they took their Bibles when you asked. He'll charge them, of course."

"Did you know?"

"No, I only knew after. Mister won't allow us in the yard. It was after he fell that we went back there. Look."

She knelt down and held the girl's wrists. Then she did the same with her ankles.

"That's how we found her. Mister had her chained to the bed."

I nodded. The girl's ankles and wrists were raw around the ends.

"In the clinic, they said Mister was asleep. They told Wezile to take him home and pray. They never say if a person has it."

"When did Vuyani get you?"

Lindiwe shrugged. "I was given to him. I'm from the farms."

Then she brushed a braid off the girl's face.

"Look, this one's even younger than me."

I nodded again. Wezile returned with the money and handed it to me wound in a thin elastic band. I counted fifties, making sure it balanced the amount.

Vuyani had fallen asleep.

"You can take him, now," I said. "He'll be awake this time tomorrow night."

Wezile nodded.

"He won't remember anything about today," I said, "but like I told you, I don't know what kind of man he is."

"Thank you," Wezile said, handing me the money for the girl.

I took it and squeezed the fifties inside the band with the rest, pushing it deep inside my pocket. It was always different with a side. There were houses that buried these girls.

I took my amulet out and pressed it down on her wound. Then I placed my fingers on her head and waited, but nothing came. I eased my palm behind her back and waited a moment longer, but nothing caught. I tried it again and she was still.

Wezile walked over to Vuyani and asked Lindiwe to help carry him to his room. Lindiwe hesitated and turned to me, but I told her to go on—I watched them hold him up by the ankles and wrists, dragging him from the kitchen like a sack of driftwood.

I touched the girl again, but nothing took. I felt surprised at the amount of effort I used. I plucked the amulet out and wiped it on both sides with my thumb. Then I ran the twine through its hole and pushed it back in again, but nothing stirred.

I sat back and watched her breathe.

In the other room, I could hear them drop Vuyani over his bedsprings.

I'd cleared her hair, I thought, revealing her crown, but nothing had worked. I could feel the heat from my illness reaching up to my ears.

This sickness often came with the job. Calls could dispense a residue inside the body, an effluvium borne from their closeness to death, which went straight to the bowels. We often prepared for this by keeping the second bucket unfilled.

I reached for mine next to the call.

On my feet again, I searched for the door.

My stomach moved in a circle behind me. I'd planned to touch them both before I got sick, but the girl wouldn't take. I didn't know why she wouldn't take.

I found the kitchen door and undid the bolt. Leaving the key in the hole, I pushed the wood against the wall. The tablecloth fell off the window, and I pushed outside to heave.

The night air cooled my sweat.

Leaning against the wall, I stood with my legs parted on the soil. Insects tittered inside the grass, invisible under squares of weak moonlight, which oozed like a thin film over the yard. The smell pierced my throat and I fumbled toward the tap.

Under the kitchen window, I released my sick into the grille.

Then I opened the tap and ran the water, splattering more vomit on the drain.

I thought about my father and how he never got sick on the job. Pa could pat his palms on a call before getting back on his feet. It was only a nip that could set him back on his knees.

There were times Pa's drinking could get the better of us. My father could walk in from a tavern with scars hatched across his forearms like a trawling net, and I couldn't keep his clothes on him when it was time to set him down for sleep.

This would happen during our winters.

Pa would kick at the walls of our box and swear, raising our pots, and then he'd begin to strip himself bare. I'd have to stoke a fire for the paraffin stove before heaving it inside. The rain would tap over the lid and the hearth and I would watch as the flames tinted the mesh dome a bright orange, a color that often put both of us to sleep.

o   o   o

CLOSED THE TAP and stumbled over the grass. Pulling the bucket to my elbow, I stood in the clear night. In the distance, on the road, I could make out the van. I was standing inside a small yard, I thought, caged by a low fence. I could see the lights burning inside the flat.

I turned back toward the kitchen.

Opening the door, I slid my arms through the crack and removed the keys. Then, dropping them in my pocket, I walked back in.

The air was muggy. I closed the girl's nightgown and pulled her over my shoulder. I could hear Lindiwe and Wezile's footsteps, the pair thumping down the hall as I closed the door behind us. Outside again, I locked the two of us out.

The girl's braids had fallen over her face, and her mouth hung open against her neck. I propped her back against the wall and felt the last dregs of nausea subside. This side is a child, I thought. Then I spat into the soil and turned back to the flat.

This was where her life had halted. I pulled her over my shoulder and started with her across the yard. I headed toward the flat, not knowing what else I hoped to find.

The girl's braids kept falling over my back as I walked, and each strand felt like the whip of a dry vine. I winced at each lash, thinking maybe they'd shriveled from a poison inside.

I could hear the door open and lock again. I knew Wezile had a spare key for the kitchen, but when I looked back, I saw the lights flicker before they blinked off.

I carried the girl across the yard.

Reaching the flat, I unshouldered her and leaned her back against the wall. Her head was tilted toward her chest, her face staring out at the open road.

They'd hung a lot of keys on the hoop. I tried the first and it picked loosely inside the lock. The second was a fit, but it wouldn't turn, and the third was too big for the hole. I tried the fourth and it caught and shifted, but it was a stubborn lock. I had to use both hands to set it loose. Then I pushed the door open, waited a moment, and turned around again.

It wasn't far from my van.

I thought of leaving the girl by the door, and then I decided to.

I was already on my way out when I turned back.

I thought of how Leonard did his work.

I didn't want to be like how Leonard did his work.

Most of us knew there wasn't much our dispatcher wouldn't do to pull a coin from the hands of a poor house. Leonard nursed a habit of fielding us calls that arrived from the men who'd done the most harm in their homes. Our dispatcher was never bothered by the state we'd find their sides in, and often he had nothing to say, either, except to tell us to hike up our fees if we felt the need to settle our stomachs.

The flat was small. It had a naked bulb, fitted sideways across the ceiling, which threw down a fluorescent light, sinking most of the shadows beneath the bed and the cabinets. The room was also clean, with stale air, a scent of polish and candle wax, and it had a bare cement floor with a single bed pushed up against a pocked wall. Next to the bed stood a narrow wardrobe: the door had been loosened from the hinges and now lay on its back against the unit, revealing a cracked full-length mirror. Lining the wall were tapered posters of soccer players, the papers gone yellow from time, below which, in a far corner, stood a blue bucket, halfway filled with water and ringed with a scatter of matches. There was no bedding drawn on the mattress. The windows had been left bare, the panes cracked between the bars.

I went back for the girl. I pulled her up and laid her over the mattress. Under the bed, I found the chains. They looked new, as if bought in time for her.

I couldn't find her clothes. I pushed her closer to the wall and sat on the edge of the bed with the chains. Then I pulled on them again, but the locks wouldn't turn.

I walked to the wardrobe. There were blue overalls hanging down from the rod, and beneath them an assortment of clothes folded in a loose pile. I pulled out a shirt with the logo of a trucking company—a gray pair of pleated pants. Then I threw them back on the pile.

The chains weren't long. I pulled on each from the foot of the bed, and both of them caught. Then, when I pulled on them again, I felt something groan against the cement.

I got on my knees and found the trunk beneath the bed. It was green and dented. The handles were padlocked to the links.

I decided to arrange the chains on the bed. I could tie them back on and touch her, I thought, but I'd left my loam on the floor inside the kitchen.

Tired, I stood up for breath.

Then I lingered for a moment.

I thought about Leonard and how he did his work.

I didn't want to be like how Leonard did his work.

I decided to take the girl back to the van, and it didn't take me long to drag us across the yard. I unshouldered her into the backseat and started the car. Then I watched my phone on the passenger seat. I had an urge to leave it dead at the call.

Exhaling again, I thought of my father.

I shifted into second and drove out to Mowbray, parking the van at the edge of the station, open for the next man on call. My breath drew a thin mist across the pane, and I reached over and wiped it, revealing a strip of lights that lined the horizon on Kewtown.

The city had droned down to silence, and I took a moment to breathe.

My father never drove himself to a fortune. Pa never stayed long enough on the city roads after taking up his calls. He'd grown up in a village, he often said, one built inside the pit of a narrow valley, a small strip shouldered by a bow of low-lying hills.

Often at dawn, a blue fog would roll down from the sides of the escarpment, and the mist would cloak itself around their doors as it moistened the windows under the thatch. Pa said this fog came down all year, and sometimes it would fall on them as thick as rain.

They used to call it the night spirit, he told me, and in the mornings, it would draw moisture from their noses for half an hour before it lifted off the crests.

Then the midday sun would drag itself over the valley and beat down on their compound: this from the dirt road that trailed out to the nearby villages and led them out to sea, and also from the rear, where the hills widened and joined the mountains that marked the start of the provinces in the north. Pa said this was his home, and one moment it was frozen over, while the other it grew so hot it appeared to be drowning.

I turned off the ignition and leaned back in the seat, not far from where I paid for my room. Then I walked out and left the car unlocked, with the keys spread out on the passenger.

Opening the gate to Ma Thano's hair salon, I carried the girl inside. I could feel the world grow still as we took cover under the back of my shed. I looked out the window as I laid her down, and I couldn't tell what it was I wanted to see: if it was my father who'd one day walk across the pane, or if it was the spirit he'd warned me of. +

MAGENTA   **PLAINS**

WILLIAM WEGMAN

March 17 - April 24, 2016

magentaplains.com

94 Allen Street New York, NY 10002   917.388.2464

METROGRAPH

No.7 LUDLOW STREET
NEW YORK CITY

metrograph.com

WHITNEY HUBBS, *UNTITLED*. COURTESY THE ARTIST.

FALLING MEN

Alejandro Chacoff

Y OU LEARNED IT QUITE EARLY ON. If someone tugged at your sleeve, or touched your back, or whiffed a kick close enough to your shin, you immediately slowed down and tripped yourself. Then you glanced at the referee and said, *"Porra, falta caralho!"* (roughly, "Fuck—foul, dammit!"). You could murmur this sentence under your breath, squint and throw your arms up in the air, and fall to the ground with the pious expression of a saint, grasping your shin and writhing with the pain of your unseen injury. Or you could just shout it so the whole pitch heard, in a crackling little whine: *Porra, falta caralho!*

It depended on what line of acting you favored. I preferred discretion. When touched on the back or gently tapped on the shin during improvised matches at school or on the hot tarmac next to my grandfather's house, I'd fall and then rise slowly, picking up the ball and placing it under my arm with a smirk of mock amusement on my face. I can't recall where I learned this style. Perhaps it was an attempt to channel the more elegant midfielders of the 1994 World Cup—the Bulgarian Hristo Stoichkov, the Romanian polymath Gheorghe Hagi. I couldn't shoot, couldn't pass, couldn't dribble, couldn't even run. I was a loathsome player. But I often dove.

My cousin, a couple years older than me, was, by contrast, admired for his skills; his father sometimes talked about sending him to Rio de Janeiro or São Paulo to try out for the big national-league soccer teams. My uncle was even more skillful, and fast on the pitch despite becoming quite stout in middle age. They dove, too.

My grandfather never played much, but he was the most obsessed with the game. In the late '70s he became chairman of Dom Bosco, a small soccer team from our hometown in Mato Grosso state. He often told me about the year they tied Corinthians at an away match in the Brazilian Championship (*Campeonato Brasileiro*)—an occasion Corinthians fans have no doubt forgotten but that my grandfather talked about until he died. By the time I was born, in 1983, my grandfather was no longer chairman of Dom Bosco. But his house was so cluttered with memorabilia, so full of newspaper clippings, desolate trophies and flags, and white-and-pale-blue jerseys, that I always thought of him as still in that line of work.

My favorite item in the house was a small golden statue of a lion that gazed out toward the horizon, its little chest thrust out. The trophy was a reference to Dom Bosco's nom de guerre: "The lion on the hill." I liked its camp sentimentality, its tackiness, the cheap gilded material from which it was made. But what I most liked and disliked about it, I now realize, was its naive derivativeness: its embodiment of that Latin American tendency to place aspiration elsewhere, to pick a foreign reference as the symbol of local truth and morality. There are many kinds of animals in Mato Grosso's swamplands—alligators, leopards, *tuiuiús* (stately birds with fine, elongated beaks), and *ariranhas* (vicious little seals that swim in packs and can maul you to death if provoked). But there are no lions in that region, and there are almost no hills.

O F LIONEL MESSI IT IS OFTEN REMARKED that he is very honest. Even if a defender rips his shirt or trips him inside the box, he'll get up and go on with the play if there's a slight chance he can score or, more nobly, assist a teammate. Such behavior lends credence to the larger myth woven around the idol: Messi, the great sportsman, the paragon of goodness; the frail boy who, suffering a setback in his early teens (he wasn't growing properly and had to take hormones), focused on becoming fast and nimble with his legs; the man who married his high school sweetheart from a backwater Argentine province like his own; who, after scoring three sublime goals in a single match and nutmegging various adversaries, mumbles a positive comment about the idle, toothpicking defenders in the back. Most of all, Messi and the act of diving are incompatible. The skill is nowhere to be found in his repertoire. To ask him to dive would be like asking Henry James to write like Henry Miller.

Most of my American friends don't understand why certain players fall at the slightest touch. The dive is something beyond their grasp. It involves two grave infringements of American morality in sports: a willingness to cheat, and the demonstration—perhaps the celebration—of physical weakness and self-pity. (The flop, basketball's closest equivalent, is less dramatic and tends to be associated with foreign players.) To be strong and athletic, full of skill, and then to break down once you reach the penalty area seems absurd. In many ways it is.

But all sports have their own peculiar absurdities, and what determines a foul always carries a certain ambiguity. In tennis, there is the foot fault—a simple and literal crossing of the line. In American football, there is pass interference, committed when a defensive player holds or pushes a receiver, or deliberately obstructs his vision of the ball while not looking for the ball himself. Pass interference is full of ambiguity and therefore open to a referee's interpretation; even mighty American wide receivers, in the attempt to win the referee's favor, have been known to exaggerate their falls.

In soccer, though, the ambiguities are endless. The field is enormous, traversed by only a few referees, and the constant melee of kicks and shoves and slides means that almost all moves are open to interpretation. Ambiguity seems constitutive of the sport. Nuno Ramos, a Brazilian visual artist and writer, often points to the difference between a soccer match's final score and the same match's possibilities; this is what gives the game such tragic and comic potential. Take the USA versus Belgium match in the 2014 World Cup, a brilliant, tense game that ended with nothing to show for it, a 0–0. There are many potentially deceitful plays in soccer—the defender raising his hands in innocence as he willfully kicks the striker's shin; the coach substituting players at the end of a match to run out the clock; the midfielder throwing the ball some feet farther afield from where he was fouled; the goalie taking a slight step ahead to increase his chances of defending a penalty kick—but the dive has gained more visibility than others. It is met with outrage where other plays are met with shrugs.

I DON'T REMEMBER when the dive started to be condemned. I think of 1994 as the landmark, if only because it's when my memories of childhood and the game converge. Back then it had been twenty-four years since Brazil had last won the World Cup, and when the great, melancholy Italian midfielder Roberto Baggio missed the last penalty shot in the final, somehow retaining his elegance while kicking the ball far beyond the bars, my mother clasped my shoulders, shook me hard, and said: "This is a historic moment you're seeing! This is a historic moment you're seeing!" The sentiment was genuine, but there was something theatrical about the way in which she expressed it; my mother never was one to make canned statements. There was something slightly off, a strange monotony in her voice.

The whole tournament had been strange. Carlos Alberto Parreira was a new type of coach, and his physical oddities—cheeks that bulged, a big slanting nose that gave him the air of a Flemish sitter—added to the strangeness of whatever he represented. The line for which he received furious criticism throughout the qualifying rounds ("The best attack is a good defense") eventually became less disagreeable, because Brazil won the tournament. But the triumph was not a pure one. Brazil, most of us now admit, played with an ugly, awkward style in that World Cup. Most matches were won by a single goal; the defense was always packed tightly in the back; the midfielders were uninspired and lazy. But for Romário's atavistic talent and reptilian lethargy—his slithering around the pitch for eighty minutes until he suddenly decided to pick the ball up and sprint headlong toward the goal—there is little to remember fondly.

Soon coaches would begin to wear taut suits and fine shoes, and Parreira, with his methodical approach to the game and simple coach's tracksuit, would start to look subdued, even humble. But the question posed by that tournament—shall one play beautifully or win?—has now haunted Brazilian soccer for two decades. The question had never been asked before; older relatives pointed out that the value of the bygone teams was precisely that they won by playing beautifully. But 1994 was different, and one sensed bigger shifts under way.

The players were becoming stronger and more physical. Even the slow ones were quick enough that they could effectively shrink the field. Short, colorful keepers, like the Mexican Jorge Campos and the Colombian René Higuita, were soon pushed out of existence; aspirants to the position now seem bred to cover the width and depth of the entire goal. Strikers kick and use their skulls with incredible force, making one wonder vaguely about the risks of head trauma. The better defenders have mastered the long pass. (Nothing irritated my grandfather more than defenders who decided they had other talents than defense to display.) Even the dribble, the skill that perhaps best illuminates soccer's artful and often inefficient character, has become less dependent on raw acrobatic skill than on horsepower: Cristiano Ronaldo's dribbles hinge mostly on his sprints, Messi's on his jittery, short-stepped velocity, the ball glued to his left foot. Dennis Bergkamp, Holland's star player in 1994 and 1998, was one of the first prototypes of this sort of powerful, efficient genius. However creative his plays, they were almost mathematically precise and straightforward. The rumor about Messi having a mild variant of Asperger's says less about him and more about the public's expectation of what a contemporary soccer genius should be.

It's hard to tell whether Parreira, who favored motivational lectures, management techniques, repetition of plays, and professionalism, was driving changes or simply reacting to them. Across countries, the game was streamlined. The long, slogging matches of the '70s and '80s, full of yawns and lulls—the defender passing the ball to the goalie and then getting it back; the striker dawdling near the adversary's goal, going offside every couple of minutes—gave way to a faster pace. It felt as if a private equity firm had bought the sport, making it slicker and more palatable to the next potential buyer. (Off the field, and in the European leagues above all, this has become increasingly less metaphoric.)

The language of pundits began to suffer alterations, too. "Tactical evolution," "tactical modernization," "finalizing capacity": it's hard to imagine my grandfather and his friends speaking in these terms. A dribble was no longer just beautiful, it was "exquisite"; a pass wasn't merely a great pass, it was "elegant" and "precise." A midfielder was not only smart—he had a "seething intelligence" and a great "articulation capacity."

The dive had no place in this new order. The cheek, panache, and amateurish quality involved in the act stood against the upgraded, sanitized version of the sport. The dive was ugly. It was a reminder of how dubious players could be, how unfair a match could turn out, how much of the game was outside one's control. And so soccer commentators, on watching a striker feign a fall around the penalty area, would invariably rejoice when the player was punished with a card. "That's the kind of attitude that has to change in Brazilian soccer," Galvão Bueno, the country's most famous, sentimental, and jingoistic commentator would say when he saw a player tumble needlessly to the ground.

IN THAT 1994 WORLD CUP, an Argentine very different from Messi had made headlines. Diego Armando Maradona—either the best or the second-best player in history, depending on your nationality—had been expelled from the tournament after drug tests revealed five variants of ephedrine in his urine. I remember his weary, haunted look at the press conferences that followed, and the vague schadenfreude one felt, as a child, watching the downfall of a rival's star. Only a few years before, Maradona had led his country to its second and last World Cup win, in 1986, and then again to a World Cup final against Germany in 1990.

Maradona the coke addict; the loquacious, profane banterer; a Peronist's dream of a boy, rising out of the slums of Buenos Aires; the Castro-loving emigré; Maradona the cheat. In the 1986 quarterfinal against England, he takes the ball around the middle of the field, sprints, and then leaves three defenders behind before dribbling the goalie and putting the ball into the back of the net. The Argentine commentator shouts in a charged voice: "I want to weep. . . . Oh God, what planet did you come from?"

But that was the second goal. The first one he'd scored that day was different. It was another goal that would go down in history, but for different reasons—the one in which he jumped and gave the ball a slight, fleeting touch of the hand while deceitfully jerking his head toward it, celebrating the goal as soon as the ball hit the back of the net. The cameras picked up the illegal touch but the referee on the field did not, and the goal counted. Asked about it by the press afterward, he said it was scored "a little with the head of Maradona and a little with the hand of God." Maradona, of course, always dove beautifully.

"INTELLECTUAL FOOTBALL-LOVERS are a beleaguered crew, despised by intellectuals and football-lovers alike," Martin Amis wrote in the *London Review of Books* in 1981. Not much has changed since then. In Brazil, intellectuals talk about soccer the way people who don't read poetry talk about poetry: with extravagant respect and a short attention span. Most soccer lovers, in turn, just ignore the intellectuals. With rare exceptions—Ramos's analyses; the staccato journalistic pieces by Tostão, a doctor and former striker for Brazil's legendary '70s squad; and the writings of Paulo Vinícius Coelho, known for his empiricist approach to sportswriting—Brazilian newspapers are strewn with columns and *crônicas* that use lofty and unimaginative soccer rhetoric: the game as a metaphor for life's unpredictability, for luck and randomness as determinants of final outcomes—ideas so vague and open-ended they could stand in for anything.

Left only to swift glances, a national sport becomes merely a screen onto which society projects its self-loathing and vanity. I grew up in what can be called a victorious soccer generation—Brazil won the World Cup in 1994, reached the final in 1998, and won again in 2002—and until the 2014 semifinal in Belo Horizonte, when the German squad annihilated Brazil 7–1, most locals seemed to live under the illusion that Brazilian soccer's superiority was incontestable everywhere. The question "Do we play beautiful or do we win?" was mainly introspective. I had to live in London for five years before I came to understand how overrated many people believed the Brazilian team to be.

The loss to Germany marked a definite change in mood. To judge by the torrent of newspaper columns that followed the match, Brazil suddenly went from the favorite to win the tournament to the most retrograde team that had ever existed—a tired, wandering specter, dazed by European supermen (the tinge of postcolonial self-loathing was impossible to miss). The loss to the Germans became an abyss into which all kinds of facile arguments were lobbed. It was the reflection of a society chronically prone to improvisation; the proof of our unwillingness to reinvent a style and adapt to global shifts. To sob at the anthem in some nationalistic paroxysm—as the players often did before each match—showed the triumph of a soppy emotionalism over rational tactics and thought. One often insightful music critic unwittingly veered into ominous, disturbing territory. "It was important that such a defeat be imposed on us by distant Germany," he wrote, "a country that expresses, perhaps better than any other, the importance of designing collective projects and seeing them through with great seriousness."

The tournament had begun for Brazil with the striker Fred falling theatrically in the box, leading to a penalty goal against Croatia. Had Brazil won the World Cup, this would have been a blip on the way to victory. But under the wider mood of self-flagellation, it became yet another instance of the country's terminal weakness, something to be excised from the national mind and punished.

I N A GAME IN WHICH almost every play demands interpretation, it's worth asking why the dive—one among many forms of foul play—has become such a focus of outrage and disgust. It's one thing to call or not call a foul; it's another to act self-righteous and show a card, as referees do, because they've decided the player is dirty. Anger over diving is essentially moralistic. If all equally deceitful plays were as strictly policed as the dive, there would be no match to speak of. "The entire game is built on influence-peddling, corruption," Ramos said in a TV interview back in 2012. "It's a kind of self-sufficient judiciary. It is not a science, nor is it a place for moralism."

The colloquial alias for a soccer referee in Brazil is "the man in black." This seems less an allusion to the black-robed judge than to the medieval executioner. Either way the referee cannot hand out his sentences at will. Try calling a single foul in that lukewarm zone around the middle of the field, where the pigeons often gather and defecate, and watch the gangs rise with their pitchforks—touching, prodding, cursing, whispering doom in one's ear. I think the most interesting curses I've heard were beside a pitch, either at the stadium or on the weekends when we watched our parents play. These were curses directed not from one player to another, but from the players to the referee. Often, when a match came on TV and the screen showed the referee's surname, my grandfather would turn and whisper to me (or maybe to himself): "Is that one for us or against us?"

He had other phrases. "It's better to win at the last minute, with an offside goal, than to beat the other team six–nil." He had a flair for mischievous statements, and this one—said casually, as though it were a platitude—confounded me at first. But soon I understood. Running a small team in the Brazilian interior had bred deep neuroses in him; a referee's decision had taken away victories or ties from Dom Bosco many times. Of the times he was favored by official decisions, though, he spoke with great pride and joy. The referee was just another variable in the great tug of narratives on the field. Perhaps this attitude discloses a conspiratorial mind-set—but, then again, mistrusting authority is hardly a bad thing. And now, two decades later, I understand him a little better. There really is something exhilarating about winning a match with an offside goal, or a badly called penalty kick, or watching your team's striker surreptitiously stick his hand out in the air to graze the ball, directing it into the net.

MARADONA SPOKE MISCHIEVOUSLY of the hand of God; Messi is now praised for being a good boy. The contrast says something about the decades that separate these two geniuses. Ramos, using the Brazilian team as his case study, connects the public's interest in purity to a class-based resentment. Scrutinizing a young player's tendency to party, drink, or fuck represents a passive-aggressive reaction by the upper and middle classes, who often feel threatened by drastic social mobility in a country for which stable and deep inequality has been the default mode for generations.

It's also no secret that the on-field puritanism of the past couple of decades is a blame-shifting strategy for corruption off the field. The influence-peddling Ramos speaks of is quite different from the backdoor dealings of FIFA, the latter being to the former as bank fraud is to petty theft at a chaotic farmers' market. Moralism need not emerge unconsciously, as an expression of national anxiety—it can be directed, pushed for, and FIFA has pushed hard for it on the field. The most commented-on image of the 2014 World Cup was not Robin van Persie's sublime header, or Götze's volley flick in the final, or even the pale, bespectacled Brazilian boy sobbing into his Coca-Cola cup as the Germans thrashed the home team (a neat symbol for the demographic granted economic access to tickets), but that of Uruguayan striker Luiz Suárez biting the Italian defender Giorgio Chiellini. As a topic of conversation, Suárez's bite was inescapable. Walking through the streets near the quay in Rio, one often ran into big, flickering screens showing Suárez in slow motion, on a perpetual loop, sinking his teeth into the Italian defender's collarbone. Everyone, from the bar owners to the rich playboys to the beggars who stood a few feet away from them on the curb, had an opinion about what should be done. "They should suspend him for ten matches," one person would say. "How is biting worse than kicking a shin?" another would answer. But the punishment didn't matter. That Suárez's bite was the scandal was a victory in itself for FIFA.

In a similar way, punishment for the dive has had the function of a show trial. The dive and its immediate aftermath have gone from a cursory occurrence tinged with a little bit of acting to a true spectacle of excess. It now has the grandiloquence Barthes attributed to wrestling. The scene is always punctuated with camp performances: the player's baffled expression on falling, the referee's slow, ponderous steps toward the player, the fiddling in the pocket for the card (red? yellow? so many options . . .). Perhaps the closest analogy is gentrification—sweeping away petty crime and dirty streets for more educated interactions and niceness. It's a distracting spectacle of sorts, a disingenuous broken-windows policy for an institution that is itself broken. Even the defensive hysteria of the uncritical gentrifier (so you'd prefer high crime rates? that everything remain dirty and neglected?) is similar to the hysteria of those who relish punishments against divers. The swiftness with which a culture accepts what was once a peccadillo as a deadly sin, though, is a more complicated process. It may involve a certain tendency to import foreign values, to imagine a lion on a hill in a swampy region where lions and hills do not exist.

The beginning of FIFA's moralistic push might be traced to the late '80s, not long after Maradona's "hand of God," with the beginning of its Fair Play campaign. A symbolic award to supposedly stimulate sportsmanship, the first FIFA Fair Play award was given in 1987 to the Scottish fans of Dundee United for their good behavior toward their Swedish counterparts, the fans of IFK Göteborg, the team who won that year's UEFA cup final. They shared the prize with the German player Frank Ordenewitz, for his decision to admit a handball in a Bundesliga match between FC Köln and Werder Bremen. The award never quite caught on—most of the public barely knows it exists—and the criteria for winning it have become increasingly vague. In 1990, the English forward Gary Lineker won it for never having received a yellow or red card during his career; in 1991, the Brazilian right back Jorginho received it simply for his model behavior on and off the field. By 1998, the award had gone political: the American and Iranian soccer confederations received it for the match they played in the 1998 World Cup without incident, and shared it with the Irish Football Association of Northern Ireland for their promotion of a match in Belfast between Cliftonville and Linfield, home to Catholic and Protestant communities.

The expression "fair play" has now become a favorite composite noun of the soccer establishment, to the point that the famously corrupt former chairman Joseph "Sepp" Blatter, upset at boos he received alongside President Dilma Rousseff during the opening ceremony of the 2013 Confederations Cup in Rio, irritably and ludicrously pleaded with the crowd: "Friends of Brazilian football, where's the respect, where's the fair play?"

In retrospect, it seems Maradona's two goals in the 1986 quarterfinal against England spawned distinct but enduring legacies. The second goal, with its fine arrangement of parts, became the Aristotelian ideal against which talented strikers would measure themselves. The "hand of God," meanwhile, kindled the FIFA Fair Play movement and contributed to a moral backlash in soccer that persists to this day.

o   o   o

IN 1990, ARGENTINA RETURNED to play another World Cup final against Germany. I was 7 years old, but I recall the adults getting into a heated argument the day of the final—an argument that extended into the evening, and that the children, my cousins and I, joined in on despite our poor understanding of tactics. The discussion that day was whether the German striker had really been fouled, or whether the penalty given—which called the match, and then the championship, in Germany's favor—was the result of a dive.

Since then, I've rewatched clips of that game. The play happens in the eighty-fifth minute—the last stretch of a match that's widely considered to be the worst World Cup final ever (violent, dull, stiff) in the worst World Cup tournament ever (it is still the lowest-scoring tournament of its kind in history). Stefan Reuter, the German midfielder, picks the ball up midfield, sprints, and holds on to it a little until his options open up. Three forwards split and widen, like a flock of geese shifting formation. Reuter's pass is precise in the way that only certain medium-range passes can be—the timing seems tailored to the striker Rudi Völler, who, shadowed by the Argentine defender Sensini, sprints into the box. As Völler receives the ball, Sensini is right behind him; the striker no sooner touches the ball than he collapses. Then there is the usual theater. Sensini gets up and turns toward the referee with that murderous expression of startled innocence. His teammates surround the referee, who, pushed and shoved, works his way toward the box and makes the irrevocable gesture toward the penalty spot. Andreas Brehme takes the kick and lands it low into Goycochea's right-hand side. Germany wins.

Had we been in the schoolyard, we would have been a little dismayed but perhaps a little delighted. Because if there ever were such a thing as a perfect dive, it would have been precisely this. The propulsion of the fall correctly measured, the context agreeably neutral, the falling not too campy—a fall so perfect that a person writing a quarter of a century later, with the ability to loop the play over and over again on a computer screen, would still, in the end, have difficulty saying what really happened.

MY GRANDFATHER LOST MONEY on soccer, and he admitted this with pride, even a little happiness. After he retired, he occasionally talked about reviving Dom Bosco, which had faced a steep, sad decline in the '80s and throughout the '90s. He spoke of the team's revival in a determined, epiphany-prone manner that betrayed his lack of faith in its ever coming to pass.

There was a man, I'll call him Alberto, who was on the board of Dom Bosco throughout my grandfather's tenure and remained connected to the team after my grandfather retired. He often came to visit, and he and my grandfather would sit together for hours drinking coffee or extract of guarana leaves diluted in water. Alberto would first speak of plans to revive the club, and then he would ask for money. He was garrulous, with strong opinions about last week's matches, who the new talents were, and who should be sacked or left on the squad. However the conversations began, they always ended the same way, with my grandfather giving him money. This went on for many years, and there was something obscene in it—one man taking advantage of the other's passion. Years later, when my interest in soccer began to fade, I couldn't bring myself to lie and feign greater interest in the game than I felt, even though I knew it would please my grandfather very much.

But there was a time when we watched many matches together. He continually asked his children to buy bigger, more modern TVs to watch them on, and each TV seemed more displaced in a room lined with Catholic shrines: St. Francis and St. Benedict, mostly. In the corner of the room was a box made of fine wood, with little glass doors that opened onto a pastoral scene. It had shepherds and the Virgin Mary, and the scene was constantly in the corner of your eye when you watched a match; it could be quite annoying. The room was often cool from the air conditioner, and it gave one a feeling of pleasant isolation. Outside, the heat was unbearable, and I associated it with movement and crowds, and the cool interior with stillness, which I preferred. I think he preferred it too. If a striker dawdled round the penalty area, dribbling aimlessly, undecided whether to shoot or pass the ball, he'd rise from the hammock on which he lay, clear his throat, and hiss: "Fall, you sonofabitch! Just fall!" +

TABLET IN PRINT:
A LITTLE BIT OF EVERYTHING

DUSHKO PETROVICH ON JERRY SALTZ

ADRIEN BOSC ON JEAN-PIERRE MELVILLE'S SUITCASE

GARY SHTEYNGART ON SHAVING

J. HOBERMAN ON CHANTAL AKERMAN'S PAIN

BRETT RATNER ON MIAMI BEACH JEWS

DAVID SAMUELS ON SALTINES

ROBERT RAND ON ANNE FRANK MANGA

BEN MARCUS, DAVID BEZMOZGIS, SEYMOUR CHWAST, DARA HORN, PERIEL ASCHENBRAND, NIR HOD, AND JEREMY SIGLER

PLUS: JELLY DONUTS, INSECURITY ARCHITECTURE, KNOCKOFF SHOES, PHONOGRAPHS, AND MATZO BREI

TABLET

CHICAGO REVIEW

59:4/60:1 (2016)

Ed Roberson:
Retrievals

including the
previously lost
manuscript
MPH,
from a 1970
cross-country
motorcycle trip

new and
unpublished po-
ems

a portfolio of
photographs

and a foldout
poster poem

To order or subscribe:
chicagoreview.org

"INSTEAD OF GOING OUT TONIGHT, DO YOURSELF A FAVOR: STAY IN AND READ THIS BOOK.

Moira Weigel and her genre-bending history of dating are excellent, illuminating company."

—Astra Taylor, author of *The People's Platform*

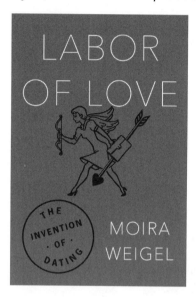

"A brilliant history of courtship, love, and sex that is also a brilliant investigation into profound changes in the nature of American work, leisure, consumer society, education, and city life over the twentieth century and into the new millennium. Elegantly written, gratifyingly clear-eyed, and sharply funny, *Labor of Love* restores the essential strangeness of dating while expertly navigating the fraught contemporary debates over its meaning."

—Nikil Saval, author of *Cubed: A Secret History of the Workplace*

Farrar, Straus and Giroux
www.fsgbooks.com

REVIEWS

A. S. HAMRAH
We're Not Ugly People
Oscar Movies 2015

The Martian

A CHILDREN'S MOVIE ABOUT HOW GREAT science is, *The Martian* has a pragmatic message for budding astronauts: you solve one problem, then another, and see if you survive. The film's obsession with years-long plans imparts a Soviet feel to the space program depicted, but its sunny optimism keeps the movie all-American. Not once do we believe *The Martian* will end with a shot of Matt Damon's skeleton half-buried in sand. Maybe the film is so bright because the days are thirty-nine minutes longer on Mars than on Earth, the same thirty-nine minutes that should have been cut from this Friday-less *Robinson Crusoe*. Kristen Wiig, however, is on hand to show that girls aren't into *The Lord of the Rings*.

Ridley Scott's backlot Mars offers a parable for New Yorkers considering the move to LA. Once you relocate, you're stranded, and the chances of getting home are remote. Yes, you'll have a vegetable garden you can sit near and watch the beautiful sunsets, but you'll be alone, 50 million miles from your loved ones. You'll conduct your social life via text and Skype, make trips to the desert in your electric car.

You'll continue to shave every day on the off-chance you get a meeting.

Room

THE MOVIES CAN PUT A POSITIVE SPIN ON anything. Seeing the world anew, or for the first time, becomes an allegory of motherhood and childhood in *Room*, which puts its protagonist (Brie Larson) in a situation not unlike Matt Damon's in *The Martian*, but earthbound, and worse. If *The Martian* is a friendly version of dark Ridley Scott sci-fi, *Room* domesticates repugnant horror with spiritual uplift. Held hostage in a shed with the 5-year-old she's had with her rapist captor, "Ma" becomes a stand-in for every young mother isolated by child care, chained by domestic servitude, and abused at night by a man who's out all day in a world she may never see again. This dismal parody of heterosexual coupling reinforces the idea that it's time to have families in some new way.

45 Years

A TOUR DE FORCE OF SUBTLETY AND RES-traint, *45 Years* is the perfect movie to see alone if you've just broken up with someone and want confirmation it was a good idea. No need to waste decades in coupledom if all it amounts to is an unnoticed gesture of frustrated defiance. The film saves that moment for its last shot, which isn't quite the indictment it's meant to be. That's because the film stacks the deck against Tom Courtenay's character, a retiree recovering from a heart attack. Courtenay's performance is a model of invisible acting, even when he's doddering or fumbling an important speech at a party, but the film belongs to Charlotte Rampling, a star presence who can command the screen just by watching the passing landscape from a boat.

The Big Short

THE PERFORMANCES IN *THE BIG SHORT* ARE carried by wigs, makeup, and bad suits, like in a silent comedy. Adam McKay, Will Ferrell's director, cuts away from everyone's big moments in their big scenes, almost walking away from them. Christian Bale, with a fake glass eye to go with his wig, moves the film along by himself for large chunks of it, often by air drumming, despite the large cast of Hollywood dudes giving it to hedge funders by playing them as self-deluded slickster oafs who will never be Ryan Gosling or Brad Pitt, no matter how many billions they sock away.

The explanatory cameos by Margot Robbie, Anthony Bourdain, Selena Gomez, and Richard Thaler barely work, and the Robbie one is a sarcastic wink-wink insult to the audience that almost tanks the whole movie while, at the same time, referring to *The Wolf of Wall Street*, a better film than this. Even though McKay gives the impression he is using recognizable forms of infotainment to educate us, the film doesn't do that—it's barely in the form of a movie. This disrespect is what makes *The Big Short* so satisfying. It jeers at and burlesques Wall Street for letting the crash happen, using Michael Lewis's book to show there were people who knew it was going to happen.

Its slapdash quality reinforces the idea that it needed to be made.

Joy

A FAIRY TALE OF LEAN-IN CAPITALISM ABOUT a Cinderella without a prince, David O. Russell's *Joy* recasts the crazy family of a Capra comedy with stellar toxicity. Joy's (Jennifer Lawrence) undermining relatives are the selfish American clan par excellence, claiming to know everything about Joy's business while sabotaging her future. Robert De Niro and Isabella Rossellini, playing evil-universe versions of themselves as Joy's father and stepmother, delight in their performances as fickle scoffers.

Joy is a natural inventor prone to epiphanies about household products—the film could be called *A Beautiful Mop.* Her ingenuity and tenacity save her from a life of drudgery, though by the end her victory seems hollow. The film, busy with fake TV soap operas and flashbacks, doesn't imagine another life for her, except maybe settling down with a cable-TV executive (Bradley Cooper) who lectures her and is wrong half the time. The mitigating factors in her struggle are that she can turn a profit, employ her friends, and help younger women manufacture improved lint brushes. Set in the early 1990s, *Joy* suggests these were the consolations working-class Gen Xers could hope for.

Steve Jobs

A SERIES OF EPIC WALK-AND-TALKS ABOUT the future retconned to be 100 percent correct because they're about our present. For example, the Amazing Steve predicts that journalism will change because of computers. (He says that in 1998, the same year

Aaron Sorkin found out.) By the end, when Super Steve tells his estranged daughter he will invent the iPod for her, the movie is indistinguishable from a TV commercial. They should have given *Steve Jobs* away for free without anyone asking for it, like that U2 album. That way, people (users) might have watched it by accident.

Sicario

A NASTY FILM ABOUT THE DRUG WAR ON THE US-Mexico border that flirts with fascism and artiness, succumbing to the former. The film suggests that the best way for Donald Trump to persuade the Mexican government to pay for a wall would be to tell them it will keep out the CIA.

Benicio del Toro, maybe the last actor from the Robert Mitchum mold, plays an Agency-backed hit man with blasé menace. Del Toro, like Mitchum, is a strange, often indifferent actor who apparently spins a wheel of fortune to choose his roles. Once he settles on one, he's either good or bad in it depending on something no one can figure out, maybe if work starts on a Tuesday. It doesn't matter who directs him. In films by auteurs like Paul Thomas Anderson and Arnaud Desplechin he can range from OK to not good, and then in an overblown thriller like this he shows up with something to prove. In some scenes he stares at Emily Blunt like he's reminding her she is not an American and doesn't work for the FBI, she's just a movie star playing a cop.

The Danish Girl

TOM HOOPER KNOWS THAT EYES ARE IMPORTANT in cinema, so he has directed the actors in *The Danish Girl* to search the corners of

NUMBER TWENTY-FOUR · WINTER 2016

STARS—THEY'RE
LEGALIZE HERO
PORN FATIGU
ON DRAKE
UKRAINE

PLUS
DAVID SA

The n+1 Magazine Reader

Subscribe to n+1? Download the entire back
catalog with our new iOS app.

$14.95US

rooms with their glances like they can't find their keys or a mouse just ran by. He makes them doll-like, ventriloquist's dummies, and when they talk to one another they converse in need-speak, as if they're explaining which line to get into at the DMV. The film begins in 1925, so Hooper has imparted a silent-movie feel to *The Danish Girl*. Everyone in this movie's Europe has been hypnotized by Dr. Caligari or tortured like Dreyer's Joan of Arc. Eddie Redmayne, as Lili, plays along, his coyness telegraphing femininity. He puts a flower between his teeth like Chaplin and seems forever on the verge of picking up two forks and sticking them into dinner rolls to make them dance. Since the film is about painters, Hooper hired Jan Vermeer to be his cinematographer.

Ex Machina

WOMEN'S CAPTIVITY IS THE GREAT THEME OF most of 2015's Oscar-nominated films, and *Ex Machina* is the most basic and manipulative of these, the tale of a hapless john sent on a bizarre mission by a pimp to see if he can free his whore. The sordidness is made oblique because the characters are a programmer, a genius CEO, and a pixie android, and it's set in a sterile underground lab. This *Taxi Driver* for nerds is heavy with the fear of superwomen empowered by data-driven emotional intelligence and synthetic physical perfection, and hence able to outflank male idiots savants. *Ex Machina* succeeds as a mindfuck stage play for three actors, Domhnall Gleeson, Oscar Isaac, and Alicia Vikander, who were in a total of about a dozen films this year, all less weird and talky than this one. The unavoidable onslaught of virtual reality and artificial intelligence will make stories like this ever more relatable to lonely techies in search

of mechanical love in robot form, but not to me. There's not even room in my apartment for a vacuum cleaner.

Creed

NOTHING BETTER COULD HAVE BEEN expected from the seventh film in the Rocky franchise than this flight from Hollywood back to Philadelphia. The savvy, intelligence, and heart of director Ryan Coogler's screenplay equals his achievement in getting an assignment like this after making *Fruitvale Station* in Oakland at age 26. Boxing movies come with built-in emotional manipulation, and this one is no exception, establishing a family for Donnie (Michael B. Jordan) by bringing back a Rocky Balboa stricken with lymphoma. Sylvester Stallone will go down in movie history as the only star of his generation willing to make way for millennials and for black America like this.

Jordan's Donnie, a pro-am boxer, rejects his status as the son of Rocky's rival, Apollo Creed, and exiles himself to working-class Philadelphia, where he cajoles Rocky into training him. When he finally puts on his father's red-white-and-blue trunks before the big fight, the moment is hokey but astute. He's forced to imitate a father who didn't raise him and who is not there to see what he's made of himself. At the movie's end, Rocky's illness is left uncured and Donnie isn't quite a champion, leaving the story ready for an eighth round. The last scene, on the steps of the Philadelphia Museum of Art, predicts the ending of *Star Wars: The Force Awakens* but undercuts its own myth.

It's clear that Coogler got cheated by the Academy of Motion Picture Arts and Sciences. Is there any doubt *Creed* was as well directed and well written as, say, *Room*? Coming a year after *Selma*'s Ava DuVernay and David Oyelowo were ignored in the Oscar nominations, ignoring Coogler was especially troubling, proof of the problem #OscarsSoWhite exposed—that the Academy consciously ignores black artists. Jada Pinkett Smith's viral video about her husband Will Smith's lack of a nomination for *Concussion* was justified, even if Janet Hubert's response video, reminding Smith that years ago he had refused to stand with other cast members of the *Fresh Prince of Bel-Air* when they wanted a raise, exposed Smith as a victim of karma. The Academy, after all, started out as a union-busting organization. He should have supported his fellow actors in contract negotiations. Yet Smith had played the Oscar game strictly according to the rules by starring in *Concussion*. It was a medical drama about a controversial subject written and directed by a conscientious filmmaker, in which Smith had to change his appearance and his accent—pure Oscar bait. If Sandra Bullock was nominated (and won) for *The Blind Side*, a sappy football drama, Smith deserved at least a nomination for a serious one.

If Will Smith, who has been loyal to Hollywood's way of doing things—loyal to a fault—can't get a nomination, what chance did Coogler have? He made a good sports drama, a big film that made money and that critics liked. The Academy told him only Stallone deserved recognition for it, the same way no one but four white screenwriters were recognized for *Straight Outta Compton*.

Straight Outta Compton

THE FIRST HALF GENERATES EXCITEMENT AS it explores teenage life in 1980s Compton and brings the group together. Then F. Gary Gray's biopic switches gears and splits Eazy-E (Jason Mitchell), Dr. Dre (Corey Hawkins), and Ice Cube (O'Shea Jackson Jr.) into a tripartite version of a Hollywood serious-composer biopic like *Rhapsody in Blue*. When N.W.A breaks up, the film becomes morose, bogged down in cameos, recriminations, and ugly management disputes—a history of beefs—before Eazy-E's sudden illness and death from HIV/AIDS brings it to a close. Eazy-E's tragedy, treated with the gravity it deserves, is not mitigated by Dre's success as a businessman or Ice Cube's prodigiousness. Cube's dignity and conscience extend to the actor playing him, Jackson, his son in real life. Jackson the Younger is a carbon copy of his father who makes him seem even greater than the original; he's somehow more Cube than Cube. Christopher Wallace Jr. set the precedent for this by playing Biggie as a child in 2009's *Notorious*, a film that didn't get mentioned much in relation to *Straight Outta Compton*, which was treated as the first biopic to admit rap's centrality to American culture, maybe because it was from the West Coast.

The Hateful Eight

I USED TO BE A MOVIE-THEATER PROJECTIONIST, and sometimes I have an anxiety dream that I'm back working in the booth. I must have been anxious about seeing *The Hateful Eight*, because the night before I saw it I had a booth dream.

In the dream, different machines are in the booth with the two regular 35 mm projectors: two 16 mm projectors set up next to two 70 mm projectors, the gauge Tarantino used for *The Hateful Eight*. These four new projectors crowding the booth—two of them small and two huge—are old models, battered and tarnished. I ask the theater manager why they're there. He tells me the director of the movie we're showing has made sections of the film in these three gauges and the movie is to be projected that way. This director has also specified what make and model of projector each reel must be shown on, down to the year it was made.

As I begin to thread the first reel, I see that the film is old and brittle and has turned pink from age. It has many torn sprockets. I examine it more closely and see it's not a new movie at all, but a western from the early 1960s by the director Joseph M. Newman. The manager tells me to get going, but when I thread the projector I put a twist in the film, which I notice after I start the movie. I tell the manager it's going to break, and he says, "Don't worry. If it breaks we'll show an old cartoon."

There were stories in the news about projectionists flying to distant cities to work in booths for *The Hateful Eight*, valiantly making sure the 70mm roadshow screenings went off without a hitch. When I saw it in 70mm in the East Village, I was happy there weren't any promos for TV shows before it, or ads for soda, or any trailers at all—they couldn't show them with a 70mm print. If Tarantino has done anything, he's given us the experience of watching a new movie by itself, on film, without any extraneous crap beforehand to remind us that movies are part of a universe of media streaming elsewhere. Sitting in that theater watching *The Hateful Eight* put me in the hundred-year flow of people in big cities watching westerns in movie theaters, dreaming of places without skyscrapers and subways.

The Hateful Eight is a reflective film in which the Hawksian Tarantino reevaluates the unfair comments he made about John Ford when *Django* came out. Maybe in rewatching some Ford movies featuring John Wayne in preparation for casting Kurt Russell in a role based on Wayne (and on the

constructed authority Wayne brought to his characters—an authority that is questioned and then eliminated in *The Hateful Eight*), Tarantino realized he has more in common with Ford than he thought. Fordian reference abounds: Russell says "That'll be the day" like John Wayne in *The Searchers*; Tim Roth's character is named Mobray, after an actor in *My Darling Clementine* who, like Roth, plays a part in a saloon; the explanatory flashback subverts the narrative *Liberty Valance*–style. The film's letter from Abraham Lincoln, Ford's touchstone in American history, proves to be false and dangerous, but a beautiful story, held till the end.

Jennifer Jason Leigh spits on that letter. She is the film's destroyer, a poisoner who exists to upend all the stories men tell one another to justify their violence. A Kali figure of the cinema, Leigh's Daisy Domergue, with matted hair and blood in her eyes, fights her captivity with a noose around her neck and the severed arm of Russell's bounty hunter—the arm of the law—dangling from her chains.

I saw *The Hateful Eight* while the occupation of the Malheur National Wildlife Refuge was happening in Oregon. *Malheur*, close to *hateful* in French, was a western, too, with a plot like Tarantino's. Holed up in the middle of nowhere in winter, a group of armed men telling one another bedtime stories about the Constitution threatened to make a bloody mess. Outside, the nation tore itself apart because a large segment of the population refused to give up old myths. *The Hateful Eight* is Tarantino's most timely film.

The Revenant

SWINGING HARD FOR THE VISIONARY AND missing, Alejandro González Iñárritu's *Revenant* combines *Andrei Rublev* with

Apocalypse Now and *Saving Private Ryan*, unfurling winter panoramas in natural light and adding CGI animals. The heart of the film, the section in which Glass (Leonardo DiCaprio) meets Hikuc (Arthur Redcloud) after the buffalo stampede, rises above Iñárritu's gory conception for a moment, before ending in a hanging and a rape, because if we forget this film's theme for a second we will be snapped back into it as punishment for daydreaming. The rest is a slog, *Klondike Kat* crossed with a Matthew Barney film, dominated by Tom Hardy's distracting-entertaining Appalachian accent. One thing is certain: Iñárritu has finally solved the problem of how to film a realistic bear fight. The next cinematic problem he should tackle is screenwriting.

Mad Max: Fury Road

TINKERTOYS IN A LANDSCAPE THAT'S LIKE A painting by Yves Tanguy, while in the foreground the Ed Roth car from the cover of the Birthday Party's *Junk Yard* album drives by at 150 miles an hour. The most cartoonish film in a year of films like Warner Bros. cartoons is also one of the best. How? *Mad Max: Fury Road* is that one-in-a-thousand reboot that will greenlight even more reboots, none of which will justify its existence like this one. Charlize Theron as a one-armed truck driver in postapocalyptic Australia wears black grease as sunscreen under a buzz cut, a look sufficiently removed from her usual perfume-ad glamour, which is displaced onto the women she is rescuing. Tom Hardy is better muttering than pontificating as he did in *The Revenant*. The entire cast seems handpicked for a kind of cinematic glory that has little to do with what goes on in other blockbusters. George Miller has done well to stay away from Hollywood and

to switch from making animated movies to live-action ones.

Miller has also remembered to make the film directly about things, not all subtext begging for explication. The scarcity of water, oil wars, the arms trade, and female emancipation jostle for space with the customized vehicles, coming in and out of focus with the blitz. But when it comes to political subtext, it must be acknowledged that Immortan Joe's demise was predictable from his water-distribution method. Pouring thousands of gallons of water on people's heads from a great height is not the best way to keep them pacified. Better to sell it to them in plastic bottles for ninety-nine cents each.

Star Wars: The Force Awakens

LIKE J. J. ABRAMS'S STAR TREK REBOOTS, HIS new Star Wars seems crowdsourced and easy to forget, an app you just closed. Kylo Ren's mask sticks in my mind because he doesn't need it and wears it anyway. He's not a disfigured monster like Darth Vader, he's handsome Adam Driver dressing up as Grandpa on Halloween, preprogrammed for redemption. He's not evil, he's just young.

Spotlight

SPOTLIGHT JOINS THE THIN RANKS OF GOOD contemporary Boston films (*Mystic River*, *The Fighter*) and does them one better by offering an explanation for the dark cloud that hangs over the place like the devil looms over the town in Murnau's *Faust*. Set in 2001, during the time of the *Boston Globe*'s exposé of pedophile priests in the Catholic Church, *Spotlight* glorifies investigative journalism and newspaper publishing for a world without newsprint. The film is spare and didactic, an instructional film explaining a disappearing profession. The editors and reporters in the film are saints whose personal lives are secondary to their work, and the Boston they work in is institutionally corrupt—cops and the courts stand between them and the truth as much as the church does.

It captures an essential truth about Boston, that feeling of drabness mixed with hostility and peculiarity anyone who has ever had to knock on a stranger's door in that town has felt. The key scene in this regard is the one in which Rachel McAdams stands at the front door of a disgraced priest, who happily admits to his crimes while his sister barks and snipes, shooing McAdams off. I'm sure that woman puts an orange traffic cone in her parking space in May.

Trumbo

DALTON TRUMBO (BRYAN CRANSTON), THE blacklisted screenwriter at the center of this earnest-frantic biopic, was pro-Soviet and a member of the CPUSA, his politics formed during the Depression. Called before HUAC in 1947, he served time in jail for refusing to name names and was denied work by the studios. After prison, he wrote films under pseudonyms, including *Gun Crazy*, and won Oscars for two of them. One was *Roman Holiday*—yes, *Roman Holiday* was written by a commie. He couldn't publicly accept or acknowledge his awards until after Kirk Douglas and Otto Preminger broke the blacklist in 1960 by giving him screen credit on *Spartacus* and *Exodus*.

As a true-life version of *Hail, Caesar!* that features many actors familiar from Coen brothers movies, Trumbo hams up the blacklist. The director, Jay Roach, directed the Austin Powers and Fockers movies, and *Trumbo* gets over its awkwardness by

focusing on the mechanics of screenwriting under duress, which Roach marvels at. Here is a screenwriter willing to risk everything, including his family, to write B movies for low pay under a pseudonym, without compromising his politics. After *Austin Powers in Goldmember*, that point of view makes sense. Actors play real Hollywood figures with varying degrees of success. Christian Berkel, who plays Otto Preminger, captures his essence, turning the combative auteur into a sly interloper popping up in Highland Park with mordant Viennese panache. *Trumbo* leaves the impression that the '50s worked out for everybody in the end, except for poor Louis C. K., as a left-wing screenwriter who smoked too much.

Bridge of Spies

ALSO SET IN THE BABY-BOOMER HEAVEN OF the 1950s and early '60s, *Bridge of Spies* presents the cold war as genteel and humane compared with the present war on terror. Tom Hanks, a high-powered lawyer but also a middle-class everyman, proves that making deals with our enemies is a better solution than building walls or dropping bombs. Retrofitting the cold war for the end of the Obama era, *Bridge of Spies* combines the negotiation of international agreements with a Trumpist approach: deals are best handled by private citizens who know better than government officials how to get what's best for the country. Today, of course, it is this businessman figure who wants to build a border wall, a bellicose reversal of this film's message.

The Coen brothers cowrote it, but Spielberg's unwavering belief in American values prevents any cynicism from coming through. At the same time, the film is mature, aware that Hanks is aging and could die of pneumonia without his overcoat from Saks Fifth Avenue. The scene with Hanks and Mark Rylance, as a pensive Soviet spy, listening to a Shostakovich piano concerto on a radio in a prison cell was not something I expected to see in a Spielberg movie.

Carol

SET IN MANHATTAN AND ON THE ROAD IN the winter of 1952, *Carol* fetishizes the mechanical equipment of surveillance—telephones, cameras, tape recorders. Carol (Cate Blanchett) and Therese (Rooney Mara), soon to be lovers, get into a dove-gray Packard to escape Carol's family but can't avoid the prying men who follow them anyway. Men are confused and pushy in *Carol*, and almost as forcibly drunk and well dressed as Cary Grant in the early scenes of *North by Northwest*. Ed Lachman's cinematography, in Super 16, is by far the most ravishing and understated among these films, a subtle tribute to the medium best suited for the intimacy of furtive glances and hushed conversations. The film is a triumph of art direction and wardrobe, a seductive art object. When Carol tells her husband, "We're not ugly people, Harge," she is telling the truth about a film that finds beauty in bad situations.

Brooklyn

LEAVING COUNTY WEXFORD, A RULE-BOUND place where shoe polish is not for sale on Sunday because it's "not a Sunday item," Eilis, a thoughtful girl played with extraordinary composure by Saoirse Ronan, sails for New York. She moves into a boarding house and gets a job at a department store in Brooklyn,

across the East River from the department store in *Carol* where Therese works in Todd Haynes's version of New York in 1952.

Eilis meets and falls in love with a handsome Italian-American plumber (Emory Cohen, channeling '50s Method actors) who's as calm and good-hearted as she is. Then she's whisked back to Ireland for her sister's funeral and coaxed to stay there by an equally kind young man played by red-haired Domhnall Gleeson, who's in every movie. Eilis almost makes the decision not to go back to the Brooklyn of 1952, a choice unimaginable to the renters of *Brooklyn* in 2016, who would take the first boat to that Brooklyn if they could. For all their strenuous effort in vintage bar and restaurant design, they watch a livable Brooklyn drift further off each day. For Eilis, Brooklyn meant freedom from the past. Somebody direct me to a place in this city, besides a movie theater, that represents freedom in the present. +

ERIN SHEEHY
Straight to Hell

William E. Jones. *True Homosexual Experiences: Boyd McDonald and "Straight to Hell."* We Heard You Like Books, 2016.

Boyd McDonald. *Cruising the Movies: A Sexual Guide to Oldies on TV.* Semiotext(e), 2015.

SUPPOSE THAT IN THE WHITE HOUSE THERE is a glory hole. That in the Supreme Court, in the New York Times Building, in the headquarters of the Motion Picture Association of America—in every place in the United States where decency is defined and defended—there is a special bathroom where people suck cock. If these cruising spots were ever made public, scandal would follow. They would be condemned, converted into sites of shame. In reality, though, they just might be the only sources of compassion and truth on the premises: a thousand points of light spread like stars throughout the nation.

"Contrary to their reputations," Boyd McDonald once said, "the real hot homosexuals who have sex in toilets and so forth are simply nicer people and more concerned, more caring, more loving, more affectionate, and friendlier than the prudes. The prudes pretend that they are the ones who are decent, and the ones in the toilet are indecent, but it's just the other way around." McDonald devoted much of his life to chronicling what the truly decent people—the ones in the toilets—were doing. A Harvard graduate and World War II vet, McDonald spent his first two decades of adult life as a "drunk and hack writer" working for corporations like Time Inc. and IBM. He found his calling in the early 1970s after he got sober, dropped out of straight life, holed up in a New York City SRO, and began publishing the zine *Straight to Hell*, a compendium of real-life gay-sex stories that is still being published today, more than twenty years after his death. Though *Straight to Hell* was mainly composed of stories sent in by anonymous contributors, it was always inflected with McDonald's own dexterous wit, radical politics, and unashamed obsession with the details of sex. *Straight to Hell* painted a world full of glory holes, where around every corner men were having every kind of sex. A reader once called it both "fantastic jerk-off material & consciousness-raising stuff."

For some readers in the '70s, *Straight to Hell* was a revelation: men were having sex with one another everywhere, all the time. It wasn't just happening in New York, San Francisco, and Los Angeles; it was happening in Pennsylvania shopping centers, Ohio taverns, and South Carolina Sears bathrooms. Vietnam vets, produce haulers, cops, "family men," octogenarians, high schoolers, priests—all were having sex with one another. They were eating shit, drinking piss, licking boots, groping each other on the subway, making out on the beach, cruising each other in broad daylight, sucking each other off.

Straight to Hell was an immensely popular underground publication. John Waters, William S. Burroughs, and Robert Mapplethorpe were fans; Gore Vidal called it "one of the best radical papers in the country." McDonald published thirteen book-length anthologies (*Meat, Flesh, Sex, Cum, Smut, Juice, Wads, Cream, Filth, Skin, Raunch, Lewd,* and *Scum*), the first of which, published in 1981 by Gay Sunshine Press, sold more than 50,000 copies. At the height of its popularity, *Straight to Hell* had a circulation of 20,000.

But for all his influence, McDonald has remained an enigmatic figure. It's easy to understand why: he was a reclusive man with a patchy history and a low social status. His work, even by today's standards, was shockingly filthy. The sex in *Straight to Hell* was neither justified nor justifiable. It was only, in McDonald's words, "the simple truth." McDonald's refusal to assimilate still feels radical in today's age of queer gentrification; at a time when people are searching for more uncompromising visions of queerness, his work is ripe for rediscovery.

IN A NEW BIOGRAPHY, *True Homosexual Experiences: Boyd McDonald and "Straight to Hell,"* the writer, artist, and filmmaker William E. Jones fills gaps in Boyd McDonald's backstory and attempts to give him a place in history. It's not easy to reconstruct

ESCAPE. DISCOVER. READ.

ON SALE MAY 3

"Mark Binelli, like Screamin' Jay himself, shouts, shimmies, and self-reinvents on the fly. . . . **Read and be moved, grooved, baited, and blued.**"
—JOSHUA COHEN,
AUTHOR OF *BOOK OF NUMBERS*

ON SALE MAY 31

"I love Helen Phillips's wild, brilliant, eccentric brain. . . . Every single story in *Some Possible Solutions* has a freshness to it that comes as a shock to the reader's system."
—LAUREN GROFF,
AUTHOR OF *FATES AND FURIES*

ON SALE JULY 5

"**Sharp-eyed and witty** . . . a delightful recipe consisting of one part girls' road trip, one part family saga, and one part good old-fashioned Southern yarn."
—SUZANNE RINDELL,
AUTHOR OF *THE OTHER TYPIST*

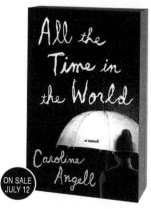

ON SALE JULY 12

"**An extraordinary book.** Caroline Angell is wise beyond her years in rendering the heartache of grief, and all the different kinds of love we are capable of feeling."
—ALICE LAPLANTE,
AUTHOR OF *TURN OF MIND*

 Metropolitan Books
www.metropolitanbooks.com

Available wherever books are sold.

Henry Holt and Company
www.henryholt.com

the story of a gay man of McDonald's era, especially one who lived such a marginal life: his contemporaries are mostly dead, he wrote surprisingly little about his personal life, and while there is an archive of his papers at Cornell University, it consists mainly of business correspondence. Jones constructs a full and fascinating biography by pulling together the little that remains, re-creating periods of McDonald's early life through local newspaper items and reminiscences from his few surviving friends and family members. Still, he sometimes comes up empty-handed: he calls one whole period of McDonald's early life—from 1958, when he left his last staff magazine job, to 1968, when he sobered up—a "lost decade." When McDonald died, in 1993, his sister and nieces knew nothing of his life as an underground porn publisher. "They say Boyd was a homosexual," his sister said to Billy Miller, the then and current editor of *Straight to Hell*, "is that true?" Overwhelmed by the volume of papers McDonald left behind, she threw everything away—the books, the magazines, the journals, the letters.

McDonald was born in South Dakota in 1925. He was drafted into the Army at age 18, and after discharge he went to Harvard. For twenty years following his graduation, he had one foot in the world of "straight" corporate media and the other in the subterranean world of gay sex in postwar America. McDonald's "introduction to homosexuality," as he put it, occurred while he was touring with a dance band right after high school, but his most formative sexual experiences were in Manhattan in the 1950s—he called it a "wildly promiscuous" time and place, and said he had sex with up to three strangers a night. It was a world of men's rooms, bathhouses, and martini bars where men had sex with each other after a long, closeted day at the office.

After graduating from Harvard in 1949, McDonald got a job working for *Time*, which was run by Henry Luce, the pro-big-business, anti-labor, and fervently anticommunist magazine magnate who'd founded *Time* with the underwhelming motto "Curt, Clear, and Complete." Jones writes that Luce looked for staffers who were "men of affirmation" rather than "men of protest"—a stifling environment for any writer, and certainly no place for McDonald. Still, many would use *Time* as a stepping-stone on the way to a respectable literary career—John McPhee and Calvin Trillin got their start there—and McDonald's long-form articles indicate that, had he wanted, he could have been a "serious" man of letters.

During this time, McDonald also contributed vivid essays and fiction to the *Southwest Review*. Though fussier than his later writing, these pieces hint at the voice and concerns that would emerge in *Straight to Hell*. In an essay about Dallas, he criticized the city's "middle-class insistence on the clean and the 'nice.'" A review of the children's book *The Book of Mother Goose* reveals his long-standing suspicion of elitist critics. "The authentic reader of the comics," he writes, conceding that a review of a children's book may seem disingenuous, "resents the pseudo intellectual who goes to Dick Tracy to achieve a comforting sense of superiority denied him in his unsuccessful reading of *Moby Dick*." But he treats *Mother Goose* seriously. "It does the two things that books must do if they are to startle many or last long," he writes. "They must offer a grotesquely unique world of their authors' own . . . and for the benefit of the readers in other worlds, they must make credible their special fictional worlds by holding them in focus with concrete detail." McDonald's own work did the same.

Though *Time* was a nightmare for McDonald, the middlebrow aesthetics, regressive politics, and clipped news-speak of the magazine later gave fodder to his satire in *Straight to Hell*. At *Time*, McDonald started out on the Miscellany column, a compilation of silly news clips with punning titles. This culled-news format later became a staple of *Straight to Hell*. In an early issue, McDonald captions a photo of a corrupt member of Jimmy Carter's administration holding his infant grandson: "Grandfather Exploits Baby."

"It was such a trauma for me, going to work," McDonald once said, "that I started drinking that very day. And I drank constantly afterward." McDonald left *Time* in 1957 and briefly worked for the IBM-sponsored magazine *Think*, after which he floated through corporate writing gigs for about a decade, sinking deeper into alcoholism. By 1968, at the age of 43, McDonald had lost his job, his apartment, and most of his possessions. Finding himself drunk and alone on Long Island, he checked into a psychiatric hospital, sobered up, applied for welfare, and moved into a single-room-occupancy hotel on the Upper West Side of Manhattan. He liked to tell the story of when he pawned all his business suits. "I remember the feeling of exhilaration," he recalled, "when I realized I couldn't have gone back into an office as a writer even if I'd wanted to."

ACCORDING TO HIS FRIEND Jim Tamulis, McDonald was first inspired to pursue erotic self-publishing after reading Gore Vidal's 1968 novel *Myra Breckinridge* and noting the titular character's interest in foreskin. McDonald placed an ad in the *Advocate*—the first mainstream American LGBT publication with national distribution—looking for men who shared his passion, and began circulating his own mimeographed newsletter, *Skinheads*, which ran letters from readers about their foreskin-related desires and their real-life sex tales. The sex stories were apparently unsolicited; it turned out that men were itching to share.

Straight to Hell was a more ambitious expansion of *Skinheads*. Approximately eight by five inches in size, the zine was packed with a diversity of reader-penned sex stories; beefcake photos; interviews, criticism and political commentary by McDonald; and clippings of "news from the straight world," such as undergraduates attacking women, priests masturbating, and police chiefs groping their deputies. This particular section was sometimes titled in German—"*Nachrichten aus der Straightwelt.*" In early issues, Jones notes, "a swastika dots the letter 'I' in most titles containing the word 'straight.'"

It's difficult to find early issues today, and due to changes in publishing laws since the 1970s, they would also be hard to reproduce. McDonald had no proof of age on file for many of the young men who appeared naked in the pages of *Straight to Hell*, and readers sent in photos of former lovers who may not have known they were being featured in a pornographic magazine. Photos of naked men with hard-ons (or "hards on," as McDonald would say) ran on the cover.

In the beginning, *Straight to Hell* was scrappy, with handwritten titles, poorly copied photographs, and profane tirades against the establishment. Jones calls *Straight to Hell* the "first queer zine," but it also prefigures hardcore punk zines: the hand-drawn elements and layout recall the art Raymond Pettibon made for Black Flag and SST Records in the late '70s and early '80s (Pettibon's work would later be featured in *Straight to Hell*). McDonald paid for printing costs with his welfare checks—he joked that it was the only gay-sex magazine funded by the US government. The zine was available via subscription and could also be found at adult and gay bookstores, but it was shunned by some of the more mainstream gay establishments—the owner of Greenwich Village's oldest gay bookstore refused to carry it.

Over the years, the aesthetic and tone of the zine softened and became more professional: photo quality improved, tirades mellowed, swastikas disappeared, offset printing and staples were introduced. But the essential elements remained the same. The zine had a recurring string of subtitles—including "The Manhattan Review of Unnatural Acts" and "The New York Review of Cocksucking"—and taglines like "The Paper That Made New York Famous" and "Always coarse, never common." Each contributor letter had a tabloid-style headline: "10 Hawaiian Dongs Unload on Tourist," "Adultery in the Men's Room," "Mechanic's Asshole Is Clean; Has Fragrance of Gasoline." Sardonic commentary on the straight world and straight press was scattered throughout; McDonald liked to run errors he found in the *New York Times*, which he considered his main competitor. Every issue featured explicit photos, sometimes in collage form. Some shots were run with permission by photographers like the beefcake pioneer Bob Mizer of the Athletic Model Guild and David Hurles of Old Reliable. Hurles photographed ex-cons and rough trade—"the state's most gorgeous goons, hoods, and whores"—which suited the aesthetic of a magazine that celebrated the working class and maintained a fascination with the straight male sex object. Other photos were sent in anonymously: a sports photographer contributed a shot of Pete Rose grabbing his dick through his baseball pants but asked to not be credited so that he wouldn't lose dugout and locker-room access. McDonald also ran interviews with marines, strippers,

smut photographers, hustlers, luminaries like Mapplethorpe, and regular joes. His wit and attention to detail were such that even an interview with one particularly terse man was illuminating:

Are your nipples the same color as your asshole? Yes. *Is your asshole like a rosebud?* Yes.

Letters composed the bulk of the magazine. They're hard to sum up; each writer had a different style and story, and McDonald took pains to preserve their individual voices. Letters were edited for length, but never paraphrased or fictionalized. McDonald left intact their misspellings, unusual grammar, and digressions. On the whole, they were candid, unrepentant, and detailed. A two-page spread in issue forty-seven features a British man with a $7\frac{5}{8}$" cock getting "impaled" by a local on a trip to Puerto Rico, a guard in Missouri receiving a surprise blow job on the night shift, a professor having sex with two truckers in the back of a van at a rest stop, and a list of transcontinental exploits from a road-tripper who'd "balled in some of the most beautiful places in the country with some of the hottest and humpiest strangers," including a Canadian Mountie in the middle of the St. Lawrence River, a Navajo ex-con at the Four Corners Monument, and a husband and wife on the lip of the Grand Canyon. Some letters were erudite. While taking Amtrak to a disarmament conference, a reader receives a hand job beneath an open copy of the *New Yorker*: "I withdrew his hand and pulled my blazer over the conspicuous blotch, the damp stigma of my delight." Other letters were barely literate: "He dropped his jean. His C was not too thick but sure was nice."

McDonald was strict about adherence to the facts. For him, the truth was more valuable than an enhanced story. It was also more erotic; that these things had really happened and could happen again was what made them a turn-on. "Any hack writer can be coherent," he said, "but these are amateur writers and they put a lot of incoherent things in. . . . The letters I like are the ones that are pretty ragged. A lot of fears and flaws, failures." The letters rarely followed pornographic convention, and many stories continued long after the climax, trailing off into the uncertain endings so common to casual sex. "We agreed to do it again but so far we've never connected," wrote one letter writer. "We went on like this for a while and then he said he had to get back to work," wrote another. "I hoped he might give me a few more moments with him but I knew that those were silly thoughts. The fact that I couldn't touch him again made me realize that we'd only had a momentary business deal and nothing more."

Some thought McDonald wrote all the letters himself. Once, the writer Stephen Greco interviewed McDonald at home and voiced doubts that the letters were real. "It was like a vaudeville routine," he recalled. "He went to a closet, opened the door, and literally out of it fell Santa Claus bags full of correspondence." If the letter writers sounded like McDonald, it was partly due to mimicry—they were, after all, devoted readers. They were also responding to McDonald's probing questionnaires, which he sent as follow-ups to letter writers whose stories lacked sufficient detail. In the 1980s, as the conventions of pornography became more widely known, men needed more instruction—not less—on what to send. "I don't want porn," he said, "but anti-porn." He wanted vivid description of "how men look, act, walk, talk, dress, undress, taste and smell," and his own personal obsessions—like the smell, taste, and general cleanliness of a man's jockey shorts—were revisited frequently.

Many letters began with compliments to a particular story or issue that the reader enjoyed, or overall praise for the magazine: "I was totally turned on by the article about the landlord & the self-abusing students," writes one reader. "If there is any justice, you are thriving and have won the Pulitzer Prize," writes another. The dialogue between readers and editor gave the magazine the feel of an intimate club. (One early issue contained the notice: "Private Newsletter. For Us Only. No 'Straights.'") It was an odd club—a cross-class, transracial effort that was unusually honest, if far from utopian. Letters like "Sucks Italian on Train" and "Cantabrigian Gets Big Surprise in Puerto Rico" featured neither the gross stereotyping of mainstream pornography nor the caution and sensitivity of today's sex-positive discourse. McDonald maintained a sharp class-consciousness in his commentary and his choice of letters. "I write for the lower and upper classes," he once wrote in a screed against bourgeois gays and their pursuit of respectability, "not the Rising Middle Class." Writers like Samuel Delany have suggested that public cruising offers a meaningful—and rare—opportunity for cross-class contact (more so than today's algorithmic cruising via app), and the pages of *Straight to Hell* support this argument. *Straight to Hell* was made for a select group of people united by their desire, but at the same time, it was a rare example of sophisticated criticism and political commentary for the masses.

McDonald saw himself as continuing the work of Kinsey. He viewed *Straight to Hell* as an important historical document: a chronicle of homosexuality in the 20th century. But he didn't strive for objectivity or expertise. He was an amateur sociologist, a private citizen exchanging correspondence with his peers—a position that offers certain advantages and partly explains *Straight to Hell*'s uniqueness. McDonald was not interested in theorizing or analyzing the stories he received. His interest was in description. His correspondence with his readers was nothing less than a massive collaborative endeavor to define homosexuality, in the sense not of fixing its limits, but of giving shape, texture, and detail to a thing so often addressed dishonestly, with condescension or euphemism.

"Gay is abstract," McDonald said. "Homosexuality is very specific, like in my books." He'd come of age in a time before "gay pride," when homosexuality was what you did in certain men's rooms, and to him the declaration of gay identity was much less interesting than what men actually did together. He said in his last interview, with the gay Boston magazine the *Guide*:

> My work is an alternative to the gay liberation movement and to the gay press. The gay press has to be sexless because they are public. And in order to be publicly gay they have to be closet homosexuals. My books are all about homosexuality rather than gayness. In other words, gay is what they are in public, and homosexual is what they are in private. My books are all about their private lives. It has nothing to do with gay liberation, gay rights, gays in the military, civil rights, fundraising, political candidates, and all that stuff.

McDonald was not on the side of the gay-liberation movement, and it was not on his. He was antiauthoritarian across the board—any public figure was necessarily a hypocrite, because respectability obfuscated the truth.

MAINSTREAM OPPOSITION TO MCDONALD'S way of life became increasingly organized—and increasingly virulent—in the 1980s, when Ronald Reagan was elected to the White House. The Meese Report pushed for lawmakers and prosecutors to crack down on pornography; the United States Supreme Court, with what dissenter Harry Blackmun called "an almost obsessive focus on homosexual activity," upheld Georgia's anti-sodomy law; and anti-porn activists on both the right and the left fought to expand definitions of obscenity. Sex began to change too, with the AIDS crisis ending much of the promiscuous public sex that had been the focus of McDonald's work. Around this time, McDonald passed editorial duties of *Straight to Hell* on to Victor Weaver, who more readily embraced the zine's popularity within the art world, throwing *Straight to Hell* parties at the Pyramid Club and Danceteria with guests like Kenneth Anger, Andy Warhol, and Fran Lebowitz. Though he had many fans, McDonald was not and never would be a part of this scene. He turned his attention to editing book-length anthologies of *Straight to Hell* (which actually brought in money, unlike the zine) and to writing more of his own criticism.

From 1983 to 1985, McDonald wrote a weekly column about movies for the gay literary journal *Christopher Street*. He claimed he hadn't seen a movie in the theaters since 1969, but he wrote about the old black-and-white films he watched on TV. His articles, published in 1985 by the Gay Presses of New York as *Cruising the Movies: A Sexual Guide to Oldies on TV*—now in a new, expanded edition from Semiotext(e)—are primarily concerned with the sexy parts of otherwise virginal films, from David Nelson's white trapeze tights in *The Big Circus* to Bomba the Jungle Boy's "chaste but occasionally fickle loin clothes."

These films, broadcast at all hours of the day on many channels (a person would need to be unemployed, and maybe an

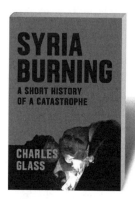

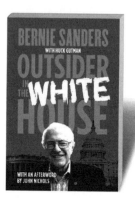

**The Killing of
Osama bin Laden**
by Seymour M. Hersh

*Electrifying investigation of White
House lies about the assassination
of Osama bin Laden*

"One of America's greatest
investigative reporters."
—*New York Times Magazine*

Syria Burning
A Short History of a Catastrophe
by Charles Glass
Foreword by Patrick Cockburn

"Tells us more about the reality
of Syria and its future than could
be gained from any other single
source." —Patrick Cockburn

Outsider in the White House
by Bernie Sanders
Introduction by John Nichols

*The political autobiography
that lays out Bernie's plans for
reinvigorating democracy*

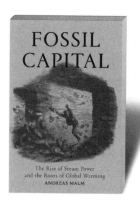

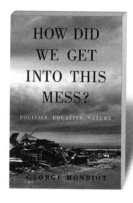

Crowds and Party
by Jodi Dean

*How do mass protests become
an organized activist collective?*

"An enthralling and exhilarating
book." – Mark Fisher, author of
Capitalist Realism

Fossil Capital
**The Rise of Steam Power and the
Roots of Global Warming**
by Andreas Malm

"The definitive deep history on
how our economic system created
the climate crisis. Superb, essential
reading from one of the most
original thinkers on the subject."
—Naomi Klein, author of *This
Changes Everything* and *The Shock
Doctrine*

**How Did We Get Into This
Mess?**
Politics, Equality, Nature
by George Monbiot

*Leading political and environ-
mental commentator on where
we have gone wrong, and what
to do about it*

versobooks.com
@versobooks

VERSO

insomniac, to catch them all), were made in the era of the Motion Picture Production Code, which from 1930 to 1968 delineated what was appropriate to show in films. At various times the code forbade, among other things, the depiction of "sex perversion," miscegenation, indecent exposure, the drug trade, brothels, dancing with "excessive body movements while the feet are stationary," and terms including "nuts (except when meaning crazy)," "hot (applied to a woman)," and, inexplicably, "hold your hat." With regard to sex, the code made a distinction between "pure love" and "impure love" and was partly enforced to prevent any stimulation of the "lower and baser element." But when you need to stimulate your baser element, you'll find stimulation anywhere. Just as one might cruise the street looking for hints about where to find sex, McDonald cruises the movies for their suggestive moments, the places where, either intentionally or accidentally, the stall door has been left ajar.

In McDonald's reviews, plots often go unsummarized; the commonly accepted "point" of movies is missed. Some articles focus solely on a single scene or shot, the fertile moment that feeds McDonald's fantasies. At times McDonald mimics the high-flown style of a serious critic, or parodies the usefulness of a *TV Guide* entry ("Paul Newman appears in boxer shorts in *Harper* [1966], seen at 4:30 p.m., September 25, 1983 on channel 1"), all the while describing men's bodies and what one might like to do to them.

Often, the articles were based on film stills and promotional photos, many provided by the now-defunct MoMA Film Stills Archive: a shot of Michael Callan's "unnerving groin" in yet another trapeze outfit, or of Gary Cooper wearing lipstick. A painted ad for *Fraternity Row* is compared favorably to an El Greco or Delacroix: the ad features a line of muscular collegians in underpants, bent over with their thumbs hooked under their waistbands as though they're about to moon a crowd. ("By excruciating use of shadow on the underpants, the artist managed to limn vividly the butt cheek and crack values inside the pants; the sensitive art lover can almost taste and smell them.")

In *Cruising the Movies*, small details open up worlds of fantasy and playful speculation. McDonald ends his essay on *The Big Circus* with twenty-four questions about David Nelson's tights: "Where did he toss his tights after a day's shooting? . . . Did he get a hard-on while dressing or undressing? . . . Did anyone in the crew whistle when he walked onto the set in his tights?" He also suggests scenes that should've been made but weren't, imagines offscreen escapades that were for some reason never recorded, and poses questions that the oblivious journalists failed to ask at the time. When David Nelson is drafted into the army in *Peyton Place*, why don't they show him getting his physical exam? In *Love Me Tender*, when Elvis Presley's big brother comes back from four years away at war, why doesn't he check out "the progress Elvis had made in growing a man-sized dick and pubic hairs"? When Elvis took David's brother Ricky aside at a party to give him advice about show business, might they have unzipped each other's pants and had a feel? *Cruising the Movies* deals with fantasy rather than fact, but it's as devoted to the specifics as *Straight to Hell*—like the imagined smell of an extra's hair tonic, or the condition of a star's underpants after a day's work.

McDonald was especially attentive to the male "suck object": he writes that Gary Cooper has the "immense dignity which comes only from being well sucked," while David Nelson "could, had he wanted, have spent his life being licked." About an extra in *Stage Door Canteen*, he writes: "even the veins of his left hand suggest that he is well wired and capable of squirting a mouthful of cream when properly aroused out of his alluring complacency." He has a special love for the actor Richard Widmark and his devastating leer: "You can say or do anything to a man who looks like that; you can feel of his fly and, a little later, unzip it. In fact he wants you to (he thinks it's good for you)."

If the letters in *Straight to Hell* were one long study of homosexuality, McDonald's own writing was often a deconstruction of straightness. (One of *Straight to Hell*'s taglines was "Love and Hate for the American Straight.") In the introduction to *Meat*, an anthology of writing from *Straight to Hell*, Charley Shively writes that McDonald's works "do not just invert middle-class values; more profoundly, they enunciate cocksucker values." In McDonald's writing, gayness is goodness and all men who aren't in some way deformed enjoy sex with other men. Inverting the sexual paradigm, he writes of heterosexuality as an aberration, an unnatural thing that must be learned, "a duty more than a desire." War, sports, and crime are the three "secondary heterosexual activities," by which men can learn and assert "straightness," which is more of a power status than a sexual one. You do not have to fuck your wife to be "straight"; a man can just as easily assert his heterosexuality through violence, which McDonald calls "a Reagan Era kind of heterosexuality, expressed through relentless boasts of masculinity and through the discharge of bullets, not sperm." If a man has sex with a male hustler but goes home to his wife, spews homophobia, and climbs on the necks of others as he ascends the ladder of respectability, who is to say he's not straight? "Straightness" does not just signify vanilla sexual interests but an alliance with the ruling elite, and a willingness to throw outsiders under the bus.

Given the bleak backdrop of the 1980s, the humor in *Cruising the Movies* can feel both dark and necessary. In a decade when homosexuality was considered synonymous with pedophilia and gay childcare workers were persecuted in the moral panic about satanic ritual abuse, McDonald calls an 8-year-old Johnny Sheffield (Bomba the Jungle Boy), who wore a loincloth and bedroom slippers to an interview, a "precocious little tease" and a "child molester's dream." At a time when the Reagan Administration was stubbornly refusing to address AIDS, McDonald suggests the President's anti-homosexual statements are just compensation for the fact he'd grown a pair of "big fat tits." Elsewhere, he calls William F. Buckley—who suggested that gay people with AIDS be branded with tattoos on their butts—one of "the nelliest men in the nation."

AT ONE POINT IN *Cruising the Movies*, McDonald suggests that the reason he receives "a barrage of butt brochures" in the mail is because the *New York Review of Books* has sold its subscription list. He calls David Nelson's butthole his "vital center," citing Arthur Schlesinger Jr. On the one hand, it doesn't matter that McDonald was a Harvard man; he himself writes that education has nothing to do with intelligence and that graduating from a prestigious university is "an economic classification and not . . . an intellectual and moral one." But McDonald's credentials help position his SRO-dwelling, pornography-publishing life as a choice, an active repudiation of respectability.

Respectability is, after all, a shield, and "serious criticism" is a good mask for insecurity or plain stupidity. McDonald praises the "confident intellectual," one who can simply enjoy Bomba the Jungle Boy instead of avoiding him on principle or pummeling him with theory. McDonald paints other reviewers as a little sad and dumb in their steadfast repression of desire, such as a *Times* reviewer who, completely ignoring a leading man's butt, "sought gratification in the picture's plot but failed," thus getting no gratification at all. *Cruising the Movies* is a corrective to all the "plot-crazed" film critics who deny one of the main roles of film: to inspire fantasy, both about the stars on the screen and about ourselves in the world.

McDonald's confidence in seeking his own pleasure in movies, as in life, was in many ways the mark of a sophisticated critic. On the other hand, his obsessions were just that—obsessive—and McDonald could be as inflexible in his worldview as he was radical. John Waters aligns McDonald's work with Valerie Solanas's, calling *Straight to Hell*, along with Solanas's *SCUM Manifesto*, "the most radical (and hilarious) filth classics in modern literature," and the coupling is telling. Though less didactic in his militarism than Solanas was in hers, McDonald was, like Solanas, an embarrassment to leftist strivers and a comic genius who, by reading society on a slant, revealed truths too damning for respectable discourse to digest.

Jones suggests that to call *Straight to Hell* the product of an obsessive crank is to dismiss the work, but the figure of the crank is a valuable one. The crank lives on the margins and sacrifices respectability in order to tell his truth. The crank doesn't chart his ideas along preexisting theories or schools of thought, but on his own experience of the world; he is driven not by the values and opinions of others, but by his own pleasures, fetishes, manias. Because the crank stays true to his own singular logic, contradictions become the texture of personality

and thought, rather than signs of hypocrisy. Returning over and over to his obsessions, the crank intellectual approaches criticism as a work of art, bringing forth his own fully realized version of the world.

At the end of *True Homosexual Experiences*, Jones looks to historical precedents for Boyd McDonald's way of thinking, writing, and living. He points to the fourth-century Greek philosopher Diogenes, who is considered one of the founders of Cynicism, and who showed utter contempt for authority, pretense, social climbing, and self-deception. He lived in a tub, "debased the currency" by counterfeiting money, and when caught masturbating in the marketplace said he wished "it were as easy to relieve hunger by rubbing an empty stomach." McDonald was a New York ascetic: according to *Straight to Hell*'s current editor, Billy Miller, he subsisted on coffee, doughnuts, cigarettes, "and maybe the occasional glass of water." Friends referred to his single room, with its tobacco-stained walls, metal cot, hot plate, typewriter, and shopping bags full of readers' letters, as monastic. Like the Cynics, McDonald was against dogma and convention, and believed in a virtue found through practice rather than theory. He preferred the honest kindness of a good blow job to any political platitudes. He held a lamp up to society, looking for an honest man—and, of course, he found him in the toilet.

THE MARKETS FOR SEX and porn have changed drastically since McDonald's day. The dirty bookstores where *Straight to Hell* was once sold have all but disappeared, and cruising has mostly moved to the internet. In recent issues, older letter writers mourn the demise of public sex. "Glory holes and O-holes between stalls were such a common thing that people just got used to it," writes a reader in San Francisco. "Now they go out of their way to plug them up. . . . It's so crazy, who's doing this and why? What's the logic? Why do they care so much about a damned hole?"

These days, new issues of *Straight to Hell* come out only once every few years. Its print run has dwindled to about 4,000 from a peak of 20,000 in the 1980s under Victor Weaver, and Billy Miller, who took over as editor in the '90s, embraces its position as a "couture object." The art and fashion worlds have become the zine's bread and butter: Miller runs special editions with limited artists' prints, takes *Straight to Hell* to art-book fairs, and is working on expanding related ventures, like film screenings, events, and merchandising. But, he says, some things aren't appropriate, and he doesn't ever want to do something that McDonald would disapprove of. "*Straight to Hell* perfume would not make any sense," he says, "unless it smelled like piss."

Straight to Hell was McDonald's obsession, and few could devote their lives to a project with such fanaticism. It now takes five people to do what McDonald once did on his own: the zine has an editor, a handful of designers, a proofreader, and volunteers to help solicit stories. Those stories are vivid as ever, though the specifics have changed: "His place smells like pot," wrote one recent contributor, "and his widescreen TV is on and a reality TV show is playing." In the latest issue, one man gets picked up in the plant section at Kmart; another reader cruises a guy in an Ed Hardy shirt at the airport. Letters continue to come in from older men, like the former marine who recalled having sex in a navy brig right after World War II, and Miller has a few men who write to him regularly from prison.

Recently, he says, he sent a copy of *Straight to Hell* to a Swiss "fashion expert." "Thank you for sending me your publication," the expert responded, "although I did not find anything in the texts or photos sexy or erotic. It's basically what my friend called 'a jerk off magazine for the poor and working class.'" Miller ran the letter in the latest issue, and says he couldn't think of a better endorsement. +

EVAN KINDLEY
Suspicious Minds

Luc Boltanski, *Mysteries & Conspiracies*. Translated by Catherine Porter. Polity, 2014.

"WHERE DOES POWER REALLY LIE, AND WHO really holds it?" the sociologist Luc Boltanski asks at the outset of his book *Mysteries & Conspiracies*. "State authorities, who are supposed to take charge of it, or other agencies, acting in the shadows: bankers, anarchists, secret societies, the ruling class . . . ?" Questions like this are not new for sociologists: an investigation of "power"—what it is, how it works, who has it, who doesn't—has been one of the dominant concerns of the social sciences for more than a century, and it has received considerable attention from historians, political economists, and literary critics as well. After Marx, Freud, Foucault, and all the rest, who could doubt that the intellectual's job is to ferret out sinister operators hidden behind the placid surface of everyday life?

Yet there's something hyperbolic, even embarrassing, about this sentiment when stated so baldly, in Boltanski's *emphatic* italics. Suspicion of the powerful is all well and good, but if one is not careful, a research agenda can easily become a paranoid obsession. Then you end up in a John le Carré novel.

In fact, Boltanski is not really asking where power lies—though he certainly would like to know. He's asking why sociologists ask the question. The similarity between the questions typically raised by sociologists and those dramatized in more than a hundred years' worth of popular fiction is the starting point of *Mysteries & Conspiracies*. It is in detective and spy stories, Boltanski argues, that we find the clearest expression of many of the paranoid attitudes and ideas expressed more apologetically and self-consciously in the social sciences and in everyday political life. The sense that the reports we hear from official sources aren't really true, that people act from motives that are secret or obscure, that a far-reaching power—call it government, organized crime, the Illuminati, neoliberalism—invisibly determines the apparently self-evident facts of our existence: these are all familiar contemporary topoi, but they have a history that stretches back into the 19th century.

LUC BOLTANSKI IS, HIMSELF, a slightly mysterious figure, at least to American readers. A star pupil of Pierre Bourdieu's in the late 1970s, he has since established himself internationally as a powerful social theorist in his own right. His idiosyncratic body of work on subjects including class formation, love, theology, decision-making, capitalism, trade unions, philosophy, the left after May '68, TV news, comic strips, and abortion has been gradually appearing in English translation over the course of the past two decades. *Mysteries & Conspiracies* is yet another surprise in an endlessly surprising oeuvre: it is, at least in part, a work of literary criticism. In it Boltanski deals with endlessly rich source material—the canon of French and English detective and spy fiction from roughly 1880 to 1970—and draws knowledgeably on scholarly predecessors

like Siegfried Kracauer, Umberto Eco, and Carlo Ginzburg. Yet despite its three-hundred-page length, *Mysteries & Conspiracies* feels sketchy and occasionally dilettantish. Like many sociologists, Boltanski is a schematic thinker who likes to craft neat conceptual categories and then slot works of art into them, and he is not much concerned with interesting anomalies or border cases. Though he discusses dozens of books by authors as various as Conan Doyle, G. K. Chesterton, John Buchan, Agatha Christie, Jack London, Maugham, le Carré, and Orwell, many of them are merely glanced at or summarized. For a book about suspicion, there's precious little close reading here.

There are also some questionable generalizations. In his desire to justify the importance of his chosen theme, Boltanski is prone to dubious statements like "Detective stories and tales of espionage . . . are the most widespread narrative forms today on a planetary scale." (As Franco Moretti convincingly argues in his 2001 article "Planet Hollywood," it's probably actually action thrillers and children's films.) And some of the local observations he makes—like the insight that detective stories never feature supernatural events, because they take place against the background of a stable social reality—are less than revolutionary.

But if Boltanski misses opportunities to dig deeper into the mysteries of genre fiction, it's because he's after bigger theoretical game. The early chapters of *Mysteries & Conspiracies*, with their talk of "formatting" reality, have a strongly metaphysical flavor. (No wonder Chesterton is one of his favorite authors.) "A mystery arises from an event, however unimportant it may seem, that stands out in some way against a background," Boltanski writes. "The mystery thus leaves a kind of scratch on the seamless fabric of reality." The "reality" in question is the one constructed by the modern European nation-state as it developed in the late 19th and early 20th centuries. The detective then becomes a kind of avatar of the nation-state, even when (as is common in English crime fiction) he is not a policeman or official state representative but an amateur, like Sherlock Holmes or Chesterton's Father Brown. "The detective," Boltanski argues, "is the state in a state of ordinary exception." That is, the detective, like the state, is always engaged in an effort to restore order, to get things back to normal: "An enigma exists as such only through reference to the possibility of a solution. . . . Once the solution has been found, everything falls back into place."

The spy's job is a little different. The difference between detective novels and spy novels is that in the former, private citizens are under suspicion, whereas in the latter, "suspicion falls in the first place on the people in power." In spy novels, the state itself often becomes an antagonist, which explains why leftist and radical authors like Eric Ambler, Graham Greene, and Thomas Pynchon have been so fond of them. The detective novel, meanwhile, has remained a primarily conservative genre. It is also in the spy novel that "suspicion, the driving force behind detective fiction, is taken to the extreme. . . . Suspicion arises everywhere and at every moment, whether or not there is an attested crime."

Boltanski spends some time with the classics of English detective fiction—in particular Holmes, whom he describes as "the detective of the worthy," whose primary job is to help members of the respectable upper classes avoid scandal (meaning, in many cases, investigation or prosecution by the state). It is Boltanski's discussions of French detective fiction, however, that are most illuminating, if not necessarily for the reasons he intends. "The Inquiries of a Paris

Policeman," the book's third chapter, centers for the most part on a single character: Georges Simenon's Commissioner Maigret. In French crime novels, unlike English ones, the detective is usually a policeman or civil servant loyal to the state rather than to the upper classes. Boltanski is at pains to demonstrate that detectives like Maigret, despite their affiliations with the state, exhibit a sort of schizophrenia—a split personality—that allows them to identify closely with criminals. This is no great shakes as a literary argument, and fans of Simenon (whose ranks have swelled in the US in recent years, thanks to NYRB Classics' translations of his novels) will not learn anything especially revealing about the character of Maigret from this account. But the Maigret sections have a special interest when read against the grain—suspiciously, as it were. Boltanski's prolonged analysis of Maigret (by far the most time he spends on any individual fictional character) can be seen as an encrypted portrait of his late, estranged mentor Pierre Bourdieu.

Boltanski and Bourdieu had a complicated oedipal relationship, marked first by intense fidelity and then by serious acrimony. In the early 1980s, Boltanski broke with Bourdieu and his disciples to form his own highly regarded sociological school, which has been called, variously, "political and moral sociology," "the sociology of critique" (as opposed to Bourdieu's "critical sociology"), and the "pragmatic" school of French sociology.

Where Bourdieu (on a certain reading, anyway) sought to unmask and denounce hypocrisy and illusion, Boltanski and his fellow travelers were more interested in studying acts of denunciation, or justification, or criticism in general. In recent years, and particularly since Bourdieu's death, in 2002, Boltanski has sought to reconcile his sociological program with his mentor's legacy—publishing a short, admiring memoir of him in 2008, for instance—but there is still a fundamental rift between the thinkers that has yet to be fully repaired.

Bourdieu is only one of many sociologists and theorists cited in *Mysteries & Conspiracies* in passing, yet his spirit looms large throughout, and especially in the detailed, ambivalent description of Simenon's hero. In his police work Maigret seeks to understand the "Milieu"—a French equivalent of the Mafia—by studying a whole galaxy of different social milieus, just as Bourdieu sought to understand the social world as a whole by launching empirical investigations into a variety of "fields":

> Like a sociologist, or a socially conscious novelist, Maigret begins by immersing himself in the milieu where the crime was committed. He identifies its hierarchies, habits, customs and implicit norms without ever passing judgement on them. His increasing familiarity with the milieu is what puts him on the murderer's trail.

This much could perhaps be said of any sociologist, but listen to these excerpts from Boltanski's extended description of Commissioner Maigret:

> Maigret is a civil servant among countless others, an ordinary person like everyone else. He is not presented as having superior intelligence; he is even somewhat suspicious of intellectual prowess and scientific methods of investigation. Born into the rural lower-middle class . . . he attended the local elementary school (and the local church, where he was an altar boy), then the lycée, as a boarder, before beginning to study medicine. . . . It was by chance and by default, not by vocation, that he joined the police force at the age of twenty-two. He

> held a modest position at first . . . then began to climb the ladder. . . . Like a sociologist . . . Maigret possesses both ordinary social competence and a specific competence that allows him to carry out successful investigations in relative independence, which means that the enthusiasm with which he approaches his task is not constrained by too much concern over the uses that will be made of his work.

Readers of Bourdieu, and especially his autobiographical *Sketch for a Self-Analysis*, will recognize many of the characteristics listed here: the son of a provincial postman, Bourdieu was born into the rural lower-middle class and studied philosophy at the École Normale Supérieure in Paris before falling, more or less by chance and by default, into sociology, a field he would go on to revolutionize and dominate. His intellectual project was founded, from the start, on a suspicion of intellectuals and intellectual prowess, an attitude many attributed to class resentment and that, by his own admission, owed a great deal to his working-class roots. He proudly acted in the capacity of a government adviser, working with François Mitterand's government to reform and "rationalize" the state educational system in the mid-1980s; yet he insisted, from first to last, on sociology's relative independence from the institutions that enabled it, whether they were governmental, educational, or corporate.

How does Maigret—who is, after all, a human being, and not just a detective—feel about his work? He struggles to remain committed to the posture of objectivity, even when that clearly goes against his natural instincts. "Isn't Maigret's motto 'to understand, not to judge,'" Boltanski asks, "a formula in which one can see the moral version of the famous 'axiological neutrality' that is the first thing taught to sociology

"Thornton is a writer of formidable talent and deep heart, and this nuanced and moving novel marks his arrival as a significant new voice in contemporary fiction."

— BRET ANTHONY JOHNSTON,
author of
Remember Me Like This

"Compelling and authentic . . . a story of China as told by an outsider."

— YU HUA,
winner of the James Joyce Award and the Grinzane Cavour Prize

"This unsettling book about the moral encounter between America and China is a study of privilege, innocence, and risk."

— EVAN OSNOS,
author of *Age of Ambition*, winner of the National Book Award

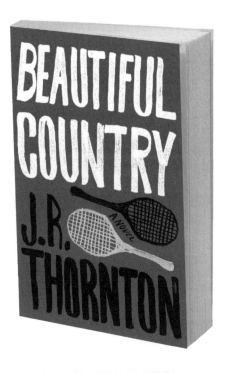

"Authentic, pure and heartbreaking . . . (Thornton) is an exceptionally gifted young writer."

— MO YAN,
2012 Nobel Laureate in Literature

"A coming-of-age story that vividly encapsulates the complexities of the modern encounter between China and America."

— NIALL FERGUSON,
author of *Kissinger: 1923-1968: The Idealist* and *Civilization*

students?" Maigret, like Bourdieu, always suspends judgment—or tries to; against ferocious odds, sometimes, he strives to remain neutral. This is especially true when he is tasked with investigating people who inhabit a social position distant from his own. "Maigret is not equally at ease in the various milieus in which he is called upon to intervene," Boltanski tells us:

> Lumbered with a heavy, slow-moving body, described as possessing characteristics stereotypical of the lower classes (he is taciturn, fond of hearty food, beer and strong drink, generous, courageous) and also some lower-middle-class traits (he likes regularity, simplicity, modest, unpretentious restaurants), Maigret is ill at ease when his investigations lead him into bourgeois milieus. The criminals he prefers because he is on the same footing with them, those who trigger feelings of humanity in him . . . are criminals from the lower classes. Simple people like himself, but who haven't been lucky; circumstances have tilted them to the wrong side.

Maigret's feeling for the unlucky lower classes is sincere, even sentimental, yet he never lets it interfere with the objectives of his profession. One thinks of the dozens of anonymous proletarians who inhabit the pages of *Distinction*, Bourdieu's landmark study of aesthetic judgment, or the immiserated masses interviewed in *The Weight of the World*, his late-career survey of contemporary poverty. Yet despite Maigret's compassion, he stays out of politics (as Bourdieu mostly did until his late-career rebirth as an *engagé* public intellectual), and avoids taking sides: it's not his job. Nor is he a liberal softy: Maigret's "anthropology," or view of human nature, which Boltanski compares to Hobbes's, is also reminiscent of Bourdieu's: for Maigret, people are driven by a relentless

desire for sex and money; for Bourdieu, they are driven by an equally relentless desire for prestige and distinction.

In Boltanski's final analysis, both men, however moral and professional they may be, have something sadistic about them: the sanguine temperament of a government torturer. They like dominating people. "This sadism," Boltanski writes,

> is never more evident than when, giving free rein to his properly human qualities, Maigret lingers over the humanity of the persons he is led to pursue, suspect, interrogate, entrap and, finally, imprison. . . . The effect of sadism is inherent . . . in the differential between the man's humanity . . . and his loyalty towards the administrative system that he serves with passion.

One thinks of Bourdieu's innumerable pages of harsh critique and vicious character assassination, undertaken and justified in the name of axiological neutrality, which nonetheless depend for their effect on something beyond objective argument: the cruelty that can't quite be justified in the name of science, the author's obvious pleasure in expertly, surgically twisting the knife.

This book about popular fiction, then, is also secretly a book about power struggles within academic sociology, over what the social sciences are supposed to prove, be, or do. The secret is out in the later chapters, which frequently leave detective fiction behind completely to expound on the themes of "paranoia" and "conspiracy theory" more generally. The largest stakes of *Mysteries & Conspiracies*, it becomes clear, have to do not with crime novels but with the legitimacy of sociological critique.

Boltanski is aware that the parallel he has set up between genre fiction and sociology is not an entirely flattering one. "Like detective fiction, and perhaps especially like spy fiction, sociology constantly tests the *reality* of *reality*, or, to put it another way, it challenges *apparent* reality and seeks to reach a reality that is more hidden, more profound and more real," he writes. Given this structural similarity, it is relatively easy for skeptics to condemn the entire discipline of sociology as a haven for paranoid fanaticism. In a bravura piece of intellectual genealogy called "The Endless Inquiries of Paranoids," Boltanski traces the development of the term *paranoia* in the social sciences, demonstrating that, while sociologists and psychologists have long used the word as an explanatory term in their conceptual arsenal, they have also frequently been accused of indulging or reflecting paranoia in their own work. "The fantasy of the conspiracy, the idea that an evil will is responsible for everything that happens in the social world, haunts critical social thought," Bourdieu once wrote, and the latter half of *Mysteries & Conspiracies* can be read as a diligent gloss on that maxim.

It is in the realm of politics, of course, that accusations of conspiracy and paranoia are most widespread, and most effective: "It would be hard to find an area today, on the margins of political life properly speaking, in which intersecting accusations of conspiracy, conspiracy theory or paranoia are not exchanged," Boltanski observes. *You're paranoid* is a way to win an argument while simultaneously positioning your opponent outside reasonable civilized discourse: in a sense, outside "reality" itself. *You're not only wrong,* the critic of paranoia says, *there's no use even talking to people like you.*

In Boltanski, this is a distinctively liberal style of argument. He deals at length with Richard Hofstadter's *The Paranoid Style in American Politics* (1964), a canonical work of midcentury American liberalism that, he

argues, did much to stigmatize all political ideas not comfortably directed toward centrist consensus as "conspiracy theories." In a celebrated passage that Boltanski quotes, Hofstadter writes of "ex-Communists who have moved rapidly, though not without anguish, from the paranoid left to the paranoid right, clinging all the while to the fundamentally Manichean psychology that underlies both."

Thus Hofstadter, Boltanski points out, establishes the "paranoid style" as "a universal model of political pathologies." Yet "what is problematic about Hofstadter's analyses," he goes on to note, "is the solidity of the position from which they are developed and whether the perspective implied in that position is external, one of overview . . . or whether it is simply one point of view among others, itself also associated with traditions, interests, and prejudices." Is "paranoia" an objective quality related to the divergence between individual suspicions and ascertainable facts, or is "paranoid" simply a name you call the people whose beliefs are furthest from your own? Liberals like Hofstadter have no interest in answering this question: to do so is, quite literally, not in their interest. But this, according to Boltanski, means that they are incapable of founding a truly sociological theory of paranoia. It's easy to dismiss those to the extreme right and left of your own position, but it shouldn't be mistaken for a scientific, or even a historical, insight.

ONE HOPES THAT ALL THIS is a preamble to some future Boltanski book that will treat the history of liberalism head-on. This isn't at all unlikely, nor would it be the first time a Boltanski book contained the seeds of the next. For someone so obsessed with categorization and schematization, Boltanski has a tendency to let the ideas in his books bleed into the margins: there are dozens of pages in *Mysteries & Conspiracies* that have nothing at all to do with detective fiction but bear on themes addressed explicitly in previous works like *On Justification*, *The New Spirit of Capitalism*, *Distant Suffering*, and *On Critique*.

Insofar as *Mysteries & Conspiracies* has a guiding thread, it's not crime stories but critical sociology, embodied in the iconic figure of Bourdieu, and those who would like to dismantle or dismiss it. "The sociologist will be reproached for taking an imaginary entity—such as 'the ruling class'—as his target, and for doing so out of a personal passion associated with political causes," he warns. "He may even be accused of producing an equivalent . . . of the conspiracy theories that nourish the resentment of 'losers,' the envious and the insane." Sociologists are always in danger of being seen as paranoids, all the more so when they oppose powerful vested interests; on this point, despite their myriad differences, Boltanski and Bourdieu agree.

In *Mysteries & Conspiracies*, as in his other recent books, like *On Critique* (2011),

we see Boltanski returning to the project of critical sociology that he and his contemporaries have done so much to call into question. How can one move beyond the endless, debilitating suspicions of a Bourdieu without settling for ratifying the liberal consensus of a Hofstadter? Boltanski himself still seems to be struggling toward an answer.

The mystery Boltanski wants to solve, ultimately, is the mystery of sociology. What is this suspicious science for? What does it allow us to know? How can it be practiced, not only responsibly but effectively? "Sociology is not a detective story," he insists, "still less a spy story, even if it sometimes tries to solve mysteries and even if it finds itself confronting the question of conspiracy." OK, fine. But what *is* it? *Mysteries & Conspiracies* doesn't solve the enigma; it doesn't even come close. But it does add a valuable chapter to the story Boltanski is writing, one that may yet end in any number of surprising ways. It confirms, yet again, that he is heir to a tradition that he is intelligent enough to realize is in decline, and committed enough to care about revitalizing. +

OUR CONTRIBUTORS

George Blaustein is an assistant professor of American Studies at the University of Amsterdam. His last piece for *n+1* was "Screw Us and We Multiply" in Issue 23.

Alejandro Chacoff is a writer living in Rio de Janeiro. His last piece for *n+1* was "No Revanchismo" in Issue 23.

Philip Connors is working on a book about mourning and megafires in the world's first wilderness. His essay "Confirmation" appeared in Issue 22.

A. S. Hamrah is *n+1*'s film critic. His last piece for the magazine was "Depiction Is Not Endorsement" in Issue 16.

Evan Kindley is a senior editor at the *Los Angeles Review of Books*. His first book, *Questionnaire*, will be published by Bloomsbury in summer 2016.

Masande Ntshanga is the winner of the inaugural PEN International New Voices Award. His debut novel, *The Reactive*, is forthcoming from Two Dollar Radio.

Sophie Robinson is a poet living in London.

Rebecca Schiff's story "Longviewers" is an excerpt from her new collection, *The Bed Moved*, out from Knopf in April. Her stories previously appeared in Issue 4.

Erin Sheehy is a writer living in New York.

Moira Weigel's book, *Labor of Love*, is forthcoming from Farrar, Straus & Giroux. Her last piece for *n+1* was "Sadomodernism" in Issue 16.

Anna Wiener is a writer living in San Francisco.

SUPPORTERS

n+1 is published with the support of the New York City Department of Cultural Affairs, and the New York State Council on the Arts.

MFA
CREATIVE WRITING
FICTION – POETRY

TEXAS ★ STATE UNIVERSITY ®
The rising STAR of Texas

Our campus overlooks the scenic Hill Country town of San Marcos, part of the Austin Metropolitan Area. With Austin just 30 miles to the north, Texas State students have abundant opportunities to enjoy music, dining, outdoor recreation, and more.

Tim O'Brien
Professor of Creative Writing

Ben Fountain
Endowed Chair 2015-16

Karen Russell
Endowed Chair 2016-18

Faculty

Fiction
Doug Dorst
Jennifer duBois
Tom Grimes
Debra Monroe

Poetry
Cyrus Cassells
Roger Jones
Cecily Parks
Kathleen Peirce
Steve Wilson

Recent Visiting Writers
Lydia Davis
Stuart Dybek
Jennifer Egan
Louise Erdrich
Jorie Graham
Terrance Hayes
Leslie Jamison
Adam Johnson
Daniel Orozco
George Saunders
Tracy K. Smith

Adjunct Thesis Faculty
Lee K. Abbott
Catherine Barnett
Rick Bass
Kevin Brockmeier
Ron Carlson
Maxine Chernoff
Charles D'Ambrosio
Natalie Diaz
John Dufresne
Carolyn Forché
James Galvin
Amelia Gray
Saskia Hamilton
Amy Hempel
Bret Anthony Johnston

Li-Young Lee
Elizabeth McCracken
Jane Mead
Mihaela Moscaliuc
David Mura
Naomi Shihab Nye
Spencer Reece
Alberto Ríos
Elissa Schappell
Richard Siken
Gerald Stern
Justin Torres
Brian Turner
Eleanor Wilner

Now offering courses in creative nonfiction.

$70,000 Scholarship:
W. Morgan and Lou Claire Rose Fellowship for an incoming student. Additional scholarships and teaching assistantships available.

Front Porch, our literary journal:
frontporchjournal.com

Doug Dorst, MFA Director
Department of English

601 University Drive
San Marcos, TX 78666-4684
512. 245.7681

CALL

FOR

PROPOSALS

MOBILE PORTRAIT STUDIO SEEKS UNPAID ASSIGNMENTS

Please send proposals for possible unpaid work opportunities.

Previous examples include:

- *costume events (incl. cosplay)*
- *livestock festival*
- *any coming of age celebration*
- *backstage*
- *family reunion*
- *sports tournament (incl. bridge)*

The Mobile Portrait Studio includes a photographer and all the gear required to print about 200 4"x6" photographs per hour. On-site!

Seeking at least one great assignment. To clarify, there is no fee.

Send proposals to:
nelson@nelsonhancock.com

LETTERS

Crystal Clutchers

Dear Editors,

I just read your piece about astrology ("Stars, They're Just Like Us!") and was reminded of a quote from one of my favorite Carl Sagan books, *The Demon-Haunted World* (1995):

> I have a foreboding of an America in my children's or grandchildren's time—when the United States is a service and information economy; when nearly all the manufacturing industries have slipped away to other countries; when awesome technological powers are in the hands of a very few, and no one representing the public interest can even grasp the issues; when the people have lost the ability to set their own agendas or knowledgeably question those in authority; when, clutching our crystals and nervously consulting our horoscopes, our critical faculties in decline, unable to distinguish between what feels good and what's true, we slide, almost without noticing, back into superstition and darkness.

P.S. I just bought my girlfriend a full set of Reiki-infused chakra crystals for Christmas.
                                        —*Nathan Curry*

On Drake

Dear Editors,

I was surprised, and somewhat dismayed, by a number of assumptions Frank Guan made in his review of Drake ("Gone Guy"), but my concern boiled down to two points, which I'll try to outline briefly.

The first was the lack of distinction made between different modes of public performance: there was little to distinguish a teenage Aubrey on Degrassi from Drake's actions onstage and online from the lyrics he raps in his songs. This seems minor, but it's crucial to understanding rap as an art form. Rap lyrics create a persona distinct from the rapper as a person, even if that persona is similar (Guan acknowledges the existence of a Drake persona, but folds it in with all the rest of his examples). As in any other genre, the lyrical persona in rap obeys and plays with conventions. That rappers, even mainstream pop-rappers, aren't 100 percent coincident with who they claim to be in their songs is an important thing to consider when holding one up as a symbol of his time.

Second, rap presents us not only with the general question of authenticity in art but with the problem of its commodification. As a middle-class black-and-white rapper, Drake appeals in part because he never hid his past (and couldn't). In his lyrics, he makes the same claims to an authentic struggle that any other rapper does; the hustle just looks different. I can't shake the sense that Guan had reduced the problem to a black-white opposition, in which if a rapper could just be "black enough," he could bust through the commodity structure of pop music, pop culture, and pop art.

When I started homebrewing in the mid-80s, my best brews were dark ales, porters and stouts. I liked the rich, chocolate-coffee flavors that came from roasted malted barley. They reminded me of malted milk balls and the hot chocolate or the malt drink of my childhood, Ovaltine. One of my most popular homebrews was called Hindy's Chocolate Stout. It contained no cocoa, but it developed rich chocolate flavors.

In the early 1990s, when Garrett Oliver became our brewmaster, we talked about developing a chocolate stout. Garrett suggested we make it an imperial stout, modeled on the beers that British brewers once created for the court of Russia's Catherine the Great. Garrett produced a test batch and called it his "resume" for the Brooklyn Brewery job. After discussing the idea with our designer, Milton Glaser, we agreed on the name, Brooklyn Black Chocolate Stout. The beer was an 11% alcohol stout with luscious chocolate flavors that immediately became a hit among beer connoisseurs. For many years, it was one of the most popular beers sampled at the Great American Beer Festival in Denver. It is still a big selling winter seasonal for us. Every year the label includes the "vintage" date. Some people store different vintages in their cellars.

Steve Hindy
co-founder

That seems false, since no one, not even Aubrey Graham (rather than Drake), can answer the question Guan poses at the end of his essay, asking whether Drake is "a black man with white social capital or a white guy with black cultural capital." It's more than fair to criticize Drake's music (including his lyrics, or his use of assistance in writing them), his means of achieving and maintaining popularity, and aspects of his life in public. But Guan collapses a lot of related but complex issues into a history of rap that betrays his own nostalgia for the period "between 1994 and 2003 [when] popular rap was, primarily and essentially, a space where young black men with nothing to lose and everything to gain by representing violence could excel." That rappers afterward—not just Drake—might play around creatively and productively with the boundaries set by the idea of the rapper as a young, violent black male seems to elude Guan as a possibility. I think that's a shame.

—*Nicole Gounalis*

Dear Editors,

I used to spend a lot of time defending *n+1* against charges of pretentiousness. "Pretentious is publishing 6,000-word articles about Lady Gaga or on the complicated cultural cross-coding of *Beverly Hills 90210*"—that was my line. Now, having read Frank Guan's epic-length assessment of an adolescent television star turned popular musician in your pages, I will either need to come up with a new argument or switch my allegiances to the *New Criterion*.

—*Ernest Vieuxtemps*

The Editors reply:

We're grateful to you for defending the magazine, but the roots of *n+1*'s pretentiousness go deeper than Issue 24, especially in the genre of music criticism—see, for example,

Mark Greif's "Radiohead, or the Philosophy of Pop" in Issue 3 (2005). We're also told that the *New Criterion* ran a very long essay on Lady Gaga and Mannerism in 2011, so you may be better off sticking with us.

Harm Reduction

Dear Editors,

I found Sarah Resnick's article ("H.") compelling and beautifully written on a subject that I certainly have my views about. As a professional in the field of drug and alcohol addiction and recovery, I have for a long time belonged to the school of "complete abstinence." Throughout my years of experience, I've seen the benefits of twelve-step recovery many times; anything short of total dedication to recovery has seemed to me worthless. I've been an avid critic of drug-replacement therapies—from methadone maintenance to the newer "miracle drug" buprenorphine—which can involve lengthy and excruciating withdrawal periods for longtime users and make getting clean extremely difficult.

Resnick's essay, however, convinced me that a harm-reduction approach might, in some situations, be a better alternative to the all-or-nothing approach. People with drug problems come from many different backgrounds and face unique challenges. A one-size-fits-all solution may thus not always be realistic. For those of us who work in addiction recovery, the best we can do is keep the door open and hope that when someone is ready to seek help, access to information—and a reminder that there is another way to live—is readily available.

What's changed in my view, having read Resnick's article, is that harm reduction may be a viable choice for those not open to, or ready for, complete abstinence and recovery.

What has not changed is my belief that recovery and twelve-step programs offer a solid path for millions of people to live happy, joyous, ethical, and productive lives free from active addiction.

—*Michael Ossip*

A Reluctant Nationalist?

Dear Editors,

As you know, I'm a great fence-sitter on Israel—this may not be particularly to my credit, but ambivalence is my disposition. So it should come as no surprise that I found Bruce Robbins's essay on BDS the most thoughtful argument for the movement I've read to date, and provoking of several nagging questions, or rather one big question that goes right to my conflicted Jewish heart.

When Robbins talks about a Palestinian "right of return," to territory lost in 1948, he seems to suggest that it is a purely strategic demand that could be exchanged, in any eventual agreement, for reparations, a tactic among tactics. "A tactic . . . is precisely what BDS is," Robbins writes. If this is true—and I wonder, first of all, how true that feeling is for the vast majority of the world's and the left's committed anti-Zionists and BDS activists—doesn't this tactical thinking perversely legitimate the logic of strategic positions on the other side? Israeli-government support for the settler movement was also reputed to be partly tactical, as seen in Barak and Sharon's willingness to give up Jewish settlements in Gaza.

By now, the tail wags the dog and settler maximalism is essentially state policy. I wonder why Robbins thinks this won't be the case with a Palestinian "right of return"? Even if I feel that the ideology of Eretz Israel threatens to become another disaster for our people, and not just in the moral dimension,

I can't wish away the idea of a majority Jewish state without also imposing on myself the responsibility of thinking about where Jews living there now will be able to go and live freely. Europe and the US's shameful handling of a mere million-plus Syrian refugees does not give me hope that one could expect great things from the international community. And I am rather perpetually shocked by the inability of most anti-Zionists to imagine a real future for Jews outside Israel. Am I becoming a reluctant nationalist?

—*Marco Roth*

Bruce Robbins replies:

I didn't say in the piece that I'm a one-stater myself, although I am, at least in theory. In practice, I suppose we have to see what we can get short of one man, one vote. But one man, one vote, in one state, would still be Israel, no? Just as whites were not asked to leave South Africa, but just to abide by the same laws as blacks. I don't imagine anyone being forced to leave.

In practice, I think the overwhelming majority of Americans who have any sympathy for BDS at all, even potentially, would feel satisfied if Israel were to retreat behind its 1967 borders and offer equal rights to its Palestinian citizens, hopefully adding an apology. In other words, I don't think right of return would be a deal breaker. Monetary compensation should certainly be offered — the Palestinians I've talked with about this (pre-BDS, admittedly) were pretty sure that would work. Even if things have changed since 2005, with the huge rightward turn in Israeli policy and the bombings of Gaza, I don't think they've changed enough to cancel that out.

It's funny you talk about becoming a nationalist. Friends on the left have called me out on hidden patriotism — but American rather than Israeli. And a couple of Israeli friends have told me my film (*Some of My Best Friends Are Zionists*) is Zionist as well as patriotic. I'm sure there's some truth in there somewhere. I'm certainly not a cosmopolitan of the totally anti-patriotic sort. Global capital being what it is, we all still rely on the nation-state more than we admit. +